Pius XII
A Saint in the Making

A Biographical Study
by *Michael Winterbottom*

UNIVERSE MEDIA GROUP LIMITED

Pius XII
A Saint in the Making
A Biographical Study by Michael Winterbottom

© Author and Universe Media Group Limited

A catalogue record for this book is available from the British Library.

Published by Universe Media Group Limited,
Fourth Floor, Landmark House, Station Road,
Cheadle Hulme, Cheshire SK8 7JH
www.totalcatholic.com

Publication date: June 2010

ISBN: 978-1-904657-65-1

Typeset in Constania by Sue Ashton

Printed in the UK by Buxton Press

*Front cover: Portrait of Pius XII by Leonard Bode. Commissioned by Sir Charles Forte.
This was the only portrait for which His Holiness ever sat. Castel Gandollfo 1957.*

In loving memory of my Mother and Father
and of Peter Schofield

"Nationalism is perhaps the most dangerous heresy of our time?"

- Papal Nuncio to Germany, Eugenio Pacelli,
future Pope Pius XII, 1923

CONTENTS

Foreword

Rome May 2010

Some time ago, Mr. Michael Winterbottom, an esteemed writer for *The Universe* Catholic weekly asked me whether I should be willing to write a short foreword to his forthcoming book *Pius XII, A Saint in the Making, A Biographical Study*. After a careful study of his manuscript, I gladly accepted his invitation because I think that publications of this type are nowadays particularly opportune and necessary. As a matter of fact, as far as the science of history is concerned, it becomes ever more clear that publications in favour of Pius XII are winning what in a recent publication was called "The Pius War."

However, while it is also true that considerable changes are taking place in what can be called the public opinion, this war has, as yet, not been won definitely. Unfortunately, in this field a considerable number of people are still unduly convinced that Pius XII was "Hitler's Pope," that he was on the side of Nazi Germany, that he was anti-semitic and for that reason he never spoke out in favour of the persecuted Jews and never did anything for them. Such opinions are, of course, completely false and patently contradicted by a wealth of documents and testimonies by Catholics and Jews who lived at the time of Pius XII, as well as by famous Jewish scholars of our present times. Nevertheless, it is obviously by no means easy to eradicate, in a short time, a more or less widespread public opinion once it has taken root on account of a systematic, anti-Catholic campaign, fueled by an efficient but as yet not sufficiently discerned and acknowledged communist propaganda.

Precisely in this situation books like the one written by Mr. Winterbottom can do an eminent service to the truth. What the general public needs today is a very readable, short but substantial account of the entire life of Eugenio Pacelli, the future Pope Pius XII, an account not limited to one or other episodes torn from the entire content of his life, an exposition not burdened by an exhaustive scientific apparatus which easily could put off readers not accustomed to this type of literature. However, lest this absence of a scientific apparatus causes the wrong impression, I wish to state that Mr. Winterbottom has evidently done very extensive studies and that indeed each of his statements can be substantiated by numerous references to documents, testimonies and other reliable sources. The value of the book is further increased by about 40 well-chosen photographs, which cover the entire life of Pius XII.

In short: I fully recommend this book and cordially wish it the widest possible diffusion, which it certainly merits.

Prof. Fr. Peter Gumpel, S.J.

By Papal appointment Autonomous and Independent Judge of Investigation for the Cause of Beatification of Pope Pius XII.

Preface

The mention of few Popes throughout history will provoke such an immediate reaction than will reference to The Venerable Pope Pius XII. Catholic and non-Catholic alike will instantly split into pro and anti-Pius camps at the very mention of his name. Few will have no opinion.

Yet this was not always the case. Immediately after the Second World War, Pope Pius was widely lauded throughout the world, statesmen and world leaders fell over themselves in heaping praise on the Holy Father, and the Chief Rabbi of Rome himself converted to Catholicism, taking the baptismal name "Eugenio" in his honour. When he died on October 9th, 1958, he was mourned the world over. President Eisenhower said "the world is a poorer place with the death of Pius XII." Golda Meir, the foreign minister of Israel, said: "Our times have been enriched by a voice which spoke the great moral truths over the tumult of daily conflicts. We mourn a great servant of peace."

So what led to the start of what has become a virtual industry, an industry with the sole aim of defaming the memory of Pope Pius XII? I hope in the coming pages to examine that industry and both the criticisms of his character and of his actions, and to a certain extent examine what motivated his detractors, some who perhaps had better motives than others.

But first it is necessary to look at just who Pope Pius XII really was, to look at his life before becoming the Supreme Pontiff, his background, what formed him and what influenced him.

CHAPTER I

"... all Rome will loudly praise this child."

Eugenio Giuseppe Giovanni Pacelli first saw the light of day on March 2nd, 1876 in his parents' third floor Rome apartment, on the Via degli Orsini. He was the third child of Filippo Pacelli and Virginia Pacelli, nee Graziosi. A brother and sister, Francesco and Giuseppina had preceded him into the world and they were to be joined later by another sister whom her parents named Elisabetta. This then was the Filippo Pacelli family at the end of the 19th century.

The whole Pacelli family, not just the Filippo Pacellis, were deeply religious, and had been in the service of the Holy See for over a hundred years. Their speciality was the law, and Pacelli after Pacelli had given their legal services to the Church. Eugenio's grandfather, Marcantonio Pacelli, had been minister of finance for Pope Gregory XVI and deputy minister of the interior under Pope Pius IX from 1851 to 1870. In his busy schedule he also found time, on July 20th, 1860 to establish the *L'Osservatore Romano*, (which to this day is still the quasi-official organ of the Vatican). He remained its editor until his death in 1902, at the grand old age of 102, while his brother Felice went one better and actually managed to live in three centuries from 1799 to 1901.

Marcantonio's son Filippo, the second of his ten children, was born in 1837. He too followed his father into the law, working for the Sacred Rota.

The Italy he lived in, however, was now a very different one from that of his father's early years, and for the first time since the Roman Empire the whole country was united. The papacy had issues with the newly united Italy.

Before the unification in 1861, the Pope was the ruler (in a civil as well as a spiritual sense) of a number of territories on the Italian peninsula. These territories, known as the Papal States, were formed in the sixth century, and over the coming centuries, as the Pope became Italy's most powerful secular ruler, as well as head of the Church, their size and authority increased accordingly. The French Revolution, however, proved as disastrous for the temporal territories of the Papacy as it was for the Catholic Church in general. The Papal States were invaded, a Roman republic declared and the Pope himself fled to France, dying in exile there in 1799. With the fall of the Napoleonic System in 1814 the Papal States were restored and until the death of Pope Gregory XVI in 1846 the Popes ruled their temporal states with full kingly authority.

The 1840s found Italy largely under Habsburg, Austrian domination, divided and fractious. When in 1848/49 nationalist and liberal revolutions broke out across the whole of the continent, Italy followed suit with another Roman republic being declared and once again the Pope fleeing the city. Though soon restored by French and Austrian troops, the Pope and the Papal States were quickly in trouble again, this time caught in the crossfire of Italian nationalism, with both sides, republicans and monarchists alike seeing the Papal States as the chief obstacle to Italian unity. In 1848 Marcantonio was one of Pius IX's closest advisors, and in 1851 became Under Secretary of Internal Affairs.

After the Second Italian War of Independence, much of northern Italy was unified under the House of Savoy but after Garibaldi's overthrow of the Bourbons in the Kingdom of the Two Sicilies, the Sardinians, fearing a southern republican government and capitalising on the general dissatisfaction with the Papal States, conquered two-thirds of them. In 1860 Bologna, Ferrara, Umbria, the Marches, Benevento and Pontecorvo were all formally annexed and by November of that year a unified Kingdom of Italy declared.

Rome was declared the capital of Italy in March 1861 but the new government was unable to take possession of the city as Napoleon III stationed a French garrison in the city in order to protect Pope Pius IX. The Franco-Prussian War, however, forced Napoleon to remove the troops in order to defend France herself. Faced with growing demands for the seizure of Rome, King Victor Emmanuel II sent Count Ponza di San Martino to Pius IX with a personal offer, offering a face-saving proposal that would have allowed the Italian army into Rome under the guise of protecting the Holy Father. Pius IX's reaction to San Martino was far from friendly and in an ill-tempered outburst declared that Victor Emmanuel would never enter Rome. On September 10th Italy declared war on what remained of the Papal States, eventually laying siege to Rome itself. Although the Pope's tiny army was incapable of defending the city Pius ordered that they should put up at least token resistance, in order to show the world that the Italians were taking Rome by force and not by consent. On September 20th, 1870 the city fell and the following October Rome and Latium were annexed to the Kingdom of Italy.

A bitter and furious Pius confidently expected the Catholic world to rally to his aid but it did not. The Italian government guaranteed to the Pope and his successors the use of the Vatican and the Lateran Palaces and a yearly income of 3,250,000 lire as indemnity for the loss of sovereignty and territory but Pius refused, claiming the necessity of independence from any political power. The former papal palace, the Quirinal, had also become the royal palace of the King of Italy and Pius withdrew into the Vatican itself, where he lived as a self-proclaimed "prisoner," refusing to leave or to set foot in St. Peter's Square.

It was against this dramatically changing political backdrop that Filippo now began building his career. As Dean of Lawyers at the Vatican he took the Vatican's battle into the secular world, twice being elected a councillor for the municipal government of Rome, where by all accounts he continued to serve the Church by defending her against the over-zealous efforts of the new government.

Filippo was also active in the work of his local church where he was a member of Catholic Action. In 1871 he married, choosing as his bride the

27-year old, by all accounts beautiful Virginia Graziosi, described by people at the time as tall, pious, graceful and well poised, "with lovely dark eyes." [1]

The social status of the family into which Eugenio was born has been the subject of some conjecture by writers. It matters in so much as the effect it would have had on the formative years of the young Pacelli. Some describe the Pacellis as grand old Roman aristocracy, the "Black Nobility" (Aristocrazia Nera). These were Italian aristocratic families who sided with the Papacy after the overthrow of the Papal States and the loss of the Apostolic Palace. Of these, families such as the Colonnas, Bentivoglios, Pallavicinis or Ruspolis, the Pacellis were certainly not a part, but at the other end of the scale to describe them as poor servants of the Vatican, living in genteel poverty, as asserted by a recent pen, is even further from the mark. Though not part of the "Black Nobility," all the Pacellis' instincts and beliefs were with them, and their life was lived to the same values. Religion and the papacy were under threat from a secular world. The Pacellis' world was the Church and the Papacy, they had and did serve it loyally from the inside, and Pacellis occupied many major and minor offices within it. And it was into this embattled world that the young Eugenio was born.

Little wonder that when raised to the pontificate, Pius XII did all in his power to raise the Church to its rightful place in the world, using all the trappings and splendours of the One Holy Catholic and Apostolic Church.

Via degli Orsini is only a short street, and leads into piazza dell' Orologio, at the far side of which is the famous Chiesa Nuova, where lies the body of St. Phillip Neri, (something of a misnomer as it was actually built in 1575 as part of a larger complex to house members of St. Phillip's Oratorian order). On the left-hand side of this street upon leaving the piazza is number 34, known as the "Palazzo Pediconi," which though never a palace, would certainly have been palatial in contrast with its neighbours, and it was in this spacious, ornate third floor apartment that the future Pope Pius XII was born.

Two days later it was to the church of Santi Celso e Giuliano that the newborn infant was taken. The church, situated not far from the Ponte

1. *Crown of Glory, The Life of Pope Pius XII*, by Alden Hatch and Seamus Walshe. Heinemann

Sant'Angelo, was the second built on the site. The first is recorded in the ninth century but was demolished by Pope Julius II, who required a new church and commissioned Donato Bramante. However, due to lack of money the design was never executed and it was 200 years later that Pope Clement XII decided to rebuild the church, this time after a plan by Carlo De Dominicis, with the project finally being completed in 1735. The small oval church was and still is a fine example of eighteenth-century art. However, its charms were lost on this newest addition to the Pacelli family who howled loudly as his priestly great-uncle, Monsignor Giuseppe Giovanni, baptised him.

A story is told, most likely apocryphal, that one of the Pacelli's clerical friends, Monsignor Jacobacci, having missed the ceremony rushed straight to the "Palazzo Pediconi." The monsignor asked to see the child, and as he held the baby, a sudden hush fell over the room. Still holding the infant, the old monsignor pronounced in a strange yet clear voice, "Sixty-three years from today the people in St. Peter's and all Rome will loudly praise this child."

CHAPTER II

"... I just tell Our Lady everything."

At five years old Eugenio was ready to start school. The family had by then made the short move to number 19 Via della Vetrina. At that time education in Italy was either state supported or religious and with the growing trend in anti-clericalism it was inconceivable that Eugenio should go anywhere other than to a religious school. So it was at a school run by the Sisters of Divine Providence that young Eugenio began his academic career. It was also situated conveniently close to home.

At that time it was not uncommon to see small shrines in all houses in Italy. The Pacelli home was no exception, except that young Eugenio wanted his own shrine and altar. It was at this shrine that he would play at being a priest, and would hold church ceremonies. At ten years old he left the Sisters and was enrolled at the private school of Professor Giuseppe Marchi. The professor had a fine reputation in Rome and his school attracted many pupils from the same background and beliefs as the Pacellis, including some scions of the Black Nobility. Situated at the far side of the Chiesa Nuova, the school was ideal for Eugenio in every respect. His intelligence and thirst for knowledge were fully catered for, he was grounded in the classics and history, and for the first time his exceptional ability to learn languages was noticed. He could soon converse fluently in French though he was, of course, to learn many more languages during his lifetime. He also displayed one of his few secular interests around this time, when he learned to play the violin and developed a passion for Beethoven, Mozart and Bach. Musicality must have run in the family as his sister Elisabetta was something of a child progeny on the piano.

On his way to and from school he would pass the church of the Gesù, inside of which there is a chapel dedicated to the "Madonna della Strada" – "Our Lady of the Way." He loved to call in to the church and pray, and once, when asked by his mother what he did for so long in the church, told her of his direct personal conversational prayers with Our Lord and Our Lady, "I just tell Our Lady everything," he said. His own church, however, was the Chiesa Nuova, and it was here, where his cousin Don Vincenzo Cirilli was the parish priest, that he became an altar boy and first assisted at the Sacrifice of the Mass, proudly wearing his cassock and cotta.

He was at this time, as he would remain throughout his life, tall, thin, and was already wearing glasses. He had an ascetic look to him, and a somewhat serious nature, though his contempories all seem to remember a none the less lively personality, though tempered by a certain frailty of health. It was also noted at the time that even in the devout atmosphere of the Pacelli household, Eugenio was growing into a more than devout child.

Despite his religious leanings, when it came time to consider his future, his father wanted his son to follow family tradition and like himself go into the law. At 15 young Pacelli had no definite idea of what he wanted to do, so following his father's advice he entered the Liceo Quirini Visconti. In 1891 this Liceo had a fine reputation for scholarship, but its ethos was quite different from the pious education Eugenio had been used to. For a start it was state controlled and the teachers at best were modernists and at the worse, anti-clerical. Liberalism and socialism were rife. The shock to the young, devout Pacelli can be imagined. His father must have known of the reputation of the school, and it can only be surmised that he considered it good for his son to be opened up to views contrary to his own. He was right to do so, for from the start something of the intellectual rigour that he was to display in later life now came to the fore, and rather than asking to be removed, which would have been understandable, instead he clinically dissected his opponents' views, and with the aid of Pope Leo XIII's encyclical *Rerum Novarum*, which had been published the year that he entered the school, he found them wanting. The encyclical and Eugenio drew sharp differences between the theories of Marx, based on his views of the class struggle, and the Christian view that led to democracy. These conclusions and views would be honed and become more sophisticated as the years went by but were in their basics never to change. He regarded communism as a specious doctrine, and a doctrine that would lead only to social turbulence. He determined to fight it, and never ceased to do so.

His flare for languages was also aided at this time by what was now being recognised as a virtually photographic memory. This never left him and in later years his ability to memorise long speeches without the aid of notes frequently astounded his staff. This, allied with a painstaking eye for detail and a lawyers' capacity for precision and evaluation were all leading to what was fast developing as a formidable mind. On a lighter note his love for music and the violin had not left him, and he would always take his violin with him on family holidays; fortunately he also excelled at the instrument, so for the listeners his performances were a pleasure and not a penance.

At the end of his second year at the Liceo, Eugenio's health began to falter. He seemed thinner than ever and had a constant cough and cold. His mother, worried about the effects of the coming winter on him, suggested he go to the small family-owned estate at Onano, and so to Onano went Pacelli, to a place where time had stood still, to dusty roads and olive groves, to peace and quiet and to a place where the hectic tempo of Roman life seemed a million miles away.

CHAPTER III

"... born to
the priesthood."

At Onano Eugenio walked, rode, swam and rowed but above all else he prayed. He had never totally decided on a career in the law, and so used his time in the peace and quiet of the beautiful Italian countryside to attempt to discern what it was that God wanted of him. His mind was suited to the law. It was a worthy career, he was following in his ancestors' footsteps, and he must have been aware of his ability to succeed in that chosen field. On the other hand, he had always had a strong draw to the Church. He was spiritual, prayerful and ever-conscious of his desire to serve and obey God. He prayed and he prayed, but he did not discern his future at Onano. Instead he returned home rested, fit, tanned and well. His family must have been delighted. However, the 18-year-old Eugenio felt the necessity for further contemplation, and applied to the Canons Regular in the Via Nomentana for permission to go on a four-day retreat at their house. He wanted complete silence and to be able to retire from the world while he discerned God's will.

After the four days Pacelli was in no doubt as to his future. God wished him to become a priest. His father seems not to have shown any disappointment at his son's decision but he could hardly have been surprised. It is equally easy to presume that his mother must have been delighted, and probably heard his decision as an answer to her prayers. To most of his family

Eugenio had simply been born to the priesthood. Now that the decision had been taken the details needed arranging. A seminary had to be chosen, and permission to enter it obtained. He also needed to be "adopted" by his bishop (accepted as a candidate) as fit to work in the diocese. All was achieved without a problem, which given Eugenio Pacelli's record and his family's history of service is hardly surprising. He duly entered the Capranica as a clerical student. The college, founded by Cardinal Capranica in 1457, was only a stone's throw away from the Pacelli home. It was a small college, with a reputation for the high quality of its education; many famous men had studied there, including a number of cardinals and a few who had even attained the Triple Tiara. Pacelli, however, had his sights firmly fixed on becoming a parish priest, and serving the people. Eugenio entered the Capranica early in November 1894. He was, at 18, older than most of his fellow students, and could have expected to spend the next four years of his life at the Capranica. The regime was strict. The students rose at 6.00 in the morning, were in communal prayer and meditation in the chapel for 6.30. Mass was at 7.00, and at 7.30 they had a spartan breakfast, followed by four-and-a-half hours of lectures, which were actually held at other colleges in Rome as no classes were taken in the Capranica itself. At 12.30 the students had their first proper meal of the day, albeit somewhat monotonous and meagre. After lunch the great continental habit of the siesta prevailed even in the seminary, and the students could relax or study in their rooms, go out if they wished (but not alone). They were in theory allowed to visit home as well but only with permission, and it was not expected that they would do so without a pressing reason. After this break there were another three to four hours of study to be taken before supper, followed by a further period of recreation, though as this consisted of discussions about their studies or theology, it was probably not looked forward to as much as their post-lunch break. Bedtime was 9.30. The routine gave Eugenio Pacelli what he most wanted in the world, time to study and to pray.

Unfortunately, a year of college added to his already frail health and proved too much for him. In later years his sister blamed the food, and throughout his life Eugenio always suffered with stomach problems. But it would seem that he also constantly caught colds and eventually developed dangerous symptoms; symptoms that the doctors feared could be tubercular. Nothing, they said, could save him apart from rest and fresh air, so it was a shattered Eugenio who retreated back to Onano. This period of convalescence must have been one of the most trying of Eugenio's life, with the feeling at times that God was not calling him to the priesthood, and he even later spoke of feelings of rejection. But once again the tranquillity of Onano, deep prayer and meditation would appear to have restored him to health in both mind and body, and it was certainly a reinvigorated Eugenio who returned to Rome. However, a return to the Capranica was ruled out as it was felt that the physical regime at the college was too much for him and indeed was to a large extent to blame for his illness.

This was a serious setback to his hopes of becoming a priest, and a solution needed to be found, and it was. Whether through Pacelli influence at the Vatican, the brilliance of the young seminarian, or a combination of the two, the unusual decision was taken to allow him to complete his studies whilst living at home. Still allowed to wear clerical garb he took up his studies once more, studying the history of philosophy at the Gregorian University, Latin and Greek at the state university of Sapienza, whilst taking theology at Sant' Appollinare (today the Lateran University).

He was eventually ordained on Easter Sunday, April 2nd, 1899, in the Church of St. Mary Major, by Bishop Francesco di Paola Cassetta – the vice-regent of Rome and a family friend in the vice-regent's private chapel. He was 23 years old. The following day in the Borghese Chapel of the same church he celebrated his first Mass.

The newly ordained priest continued his studies and having obtained a doctorate in theology, went on to obtain a second doctorate in canon law and civil law from the Apollinare. At the same time he also became curate at the Chiesa Nuova, the same church where he had served as an altar boy. He naturally fulfilled all the duties expected of a curate, hearing confession, saying Mass, teaching catechism, and visiting the sick, but he also became spiritual counsellor to the pupils of the Cenacle Convent in Rome. Young Father Pacelli had achieved his life ambition and was now caring for the spiritual needs of God's people.

CHAPTER IV

"... a knock at the door."

There seems to be little or no dissent to the view that Fr. Pacelli saw his future and indeed his calling as the care of souls, and in pastoral work. This view is borne out by his sister Elisabetta, who remembered that late one evening in 1901, whilst accompanying Euganio's violin playing, on her mandolin, there was a knock at the door, and to their amazement there stood Monsignor Pietro Gasparri, the recently appointed secretary at the Department of Extraordinary Ecclesiastical Affairs (Foreign Office), of the Vatican.

Pietro Gasparri was 53-years-old when he paid his visit to young Fr. Pacelli. He was descended from a family of shepherds, and his brilliance as a canon lawyer was of world renown. For the previous 18 years he had held the chair of canon law at the Institut Catholique in Paris. The purpose of his visit was a simple one; he had come to recruit Eugenio to work with him at the Department of Extraordinary Ecclesiastical Affairs. Pacelli was amazed and seemed unaware that the Vatican had noticed his talents. He refused and protested his wish to continue with his pastoral duties, but Gasparri insisted, and no doubt using all his, not inconsiderable, diplomatic and persuasive skills persuaded Eugenio that his particular skills were needed by the Church herself. It seems likely that he also promised the young priest that time would still be found for him to undertake pastoral duties in the parish. Eugenio relented. From that moment on Pacelli's life changed completely, no more the young curate, with a care of souls, but a part of the Vatican's well-oiled administrative machine.

Looking at Eugenio's career in the Diplomatic Service it is clear that from the very start his outstanding intellect and ability had him marked out for a "fast track" career. It started in the first few months of his arrival when, in January 1901, Queen Victoria died, and Pope Leo XIII chose him to carry his personal condolences to the new King, Edward VII. He was still only 25 years old. And this was his first taste of international diplomacy.

In 1903 Leo XIII died, genuinely mourned by all, his mark on the Church was widely recognised as being one of rejuvenation. Vatican staff, especially those in the Foreign Office, were hoping that Cardinal Secretary of State Rampolla would be elected in his place, and he was indeed everyone's favourite to succeed. On the first ballot at the ensuing conclave Cardinal Rampolla received 24 votes, Cardinal Gotti had 17 and Cardinal Sarto five votes. On the second ballot, Rampolla had gained a further five votes, as had Sarto. The next day it seemed that Rampolla would be elected, but a day of high drama was about to unfold. It started when Polish Cardinal Jan Puzyna stood and addressed his fellow cardinals: "I am honoured to present a memorandum from His Apostolic Majesty Emperor Franz-Joseph of Austria, King of Hungary." He then went on to declare a veto (*jus exclusivae*) against Rampolla's nomination. This much disputed right had been claimed by Catholic monarchs for centuries, and though never actually agreed by the Holy See, it had never been denied. In this case it is now widely believed that the veto was inspired by the Italian government, who feared Rampolla's ability and outspokenness. Many among the conclave, including Rampolla, protested the veto, and it was even suggested that he be elected Pope despite it.

However, the third vote had already begun, and the conclave had to continue with the voting, which resulted in no clear winner, though it did indicate that many of the conclave now wished to turn their support to Sarto, who had 21 votes when counted. The fourth vote showed Rampolla with 30 votes and Sarto with 24. It seemed clear that the cardinals were moving toward Cardinal Sarto.

The following morning the fifth vote of the conclave was taken, and the count had Rampolla with ten votes, Gotti with two and Sarto with 50 votes. Thus, on August 4th, 1903, Cardinal Sarto was elected the 257th pontiff. This also marked the last time a veto would be exercised by a Catholic monarch in the proceedings of the conclave.

Giuseppe Melchiorre Sarto was born on June 2nd, 1835 at Treviso in Italy. His father was the village postman but it was from his mother, Margarita Sanson, that he received a profoundly Christian influence which led him, after successful studies in the college at Castelfranco, to the seminary at Padua in 1850. His exceptional mind soon became evident, along with "the eminent distinction of his spirit." He took the name of Pius, the tenth of that name, and was, in many ways, the ideal man to continue with the work started by his predecessor Leo XIII. Leo had actively promoted a link between the Catholic Church and secular culture; faith and science; and divine revelation and reason. From the very start Pius X defended the Catholic faith against popular 19th century views such as indifferentism and relativism, which his predecessors had equally warned against. He also followed his predecessor's example by promoting Thomas Aquinas and Thomism as the only theology to be taught in Catholic institutions. This must have been music to Eugenio Pacelli's ears as he had the same deeply held belief.

Back at the Vatican, although still a fairly humble *minutante*, roughly the equivalent of a confidential secretary, Eugenio had quickly begun to accumulate a vast knowledge of international affairs. Here his legal training, which he had feared were wasted years, now stood him in good stead and his reports and judgements were recognised as being particularly penetrative and precise. With this legal training and acute mind he was also a natural choice to work on the vast codification of canon law. The huge task of codifying thousands of years of documents, papal bulls, decrees and regulations was begun under the papacy of Pius X, and in 1904 was expected to require 25 years to complete. However Gasparri, with Pacelli working under him, managed to hand over the first printed copy of the new Code of Canon Law on December 4th, 1916. It was solemnly promulgated on Pentecost 1917. Gasparri had also been elevated to the cardinalate in December 1907.

Pacelli too had received promotion. In 1904 he became a Papal Chamberlain with the title of Monsignor; one year later a Domestic Prelate to His Holiness. However, he still found time to work at the Chiesa Nuova, as promised by Cardinal Gasparri, continuing to teach catechism, hear confessions and occasionally preach; he conducted spiritual conferences for the French Sisters of Namur who ran an academy for girls of the Roman aristocracy, and became a part-time lecturer in canon law at his old college, the Apollinare.

One of Pius X's first acts on being elected Supreme Pontiff was to appoint a new Secretary of State, one Rafael Merry del Val y Zulueta whom he also elevated to the cardinalate. Merry del Val was the scion of an old Aristocratic Spanish family. His mother was an Englishwoman, and he had been born in England, and mostly educated there.

His English was, of course, fluent. His father, the Marquis Merry del Val, had been Spanish Ambassador to the Vatican, and his brother represented Spain at the Court of St. James from 1913 to 1931. He had been educated at the seminary at Ushaw in Durham, but went to Rome to finish his studies, eventually being ordained for work in the Diocese of Westminster. However, the Vatican chose to keep him in the service of the Holy See, where he soon became one of the most astute diplomats they had. Now at 37 he was the youngest man ever to be appointed Cardinal Secretary of State.

In 1908 the young Monsignor Pacelli was once again sent to England, this time as assistant to Cardinal Merry del Val at the first International Eucharistic Congress to be held in Britain, and then in 1911 he found himself once again in England as a member of the Papal delegation for the coronation of King George V and Queen Mary. In what was fast becoming a momentous year for him he was also offered the post of Professor of Roman Law at the Catholic University of America in Washington. The Pope and Cardinal Merry del Val, however, requested that he refuse the offer. What the offer clearly shows is just how much his reputation had started to spread around the world. Nearer to home his star also continued in the ascent, for in the same year he was appointed Assistant Secretary of State, the following year pro-Secretary of State, and in 1914 the Secretary of the Congregation for Extraordinary Ecclesiastical Affairs, replacing Cardinal Gasparri, who had been made Vatican Secretary of State.

Filippo Pacelli

Virginia Pacelli

The room in which Eugenio Pacelli was born on March 2nd, 1876

The drawing room at 34, "Palazzo Pediconi" Via degli Orsini

Eugenio Pacelli's desk at home

Eugenio aged 6

The Church of SS Celso and Julian, where the infant Eugenio was baptised by his uncle Monsignor Giuseppe Giovanni

Pictured above and below, The Church of Santa Maria in Vallicella, (Chiesa Nuova), where the young Eugenio would call and "tell Our Lady everything," where he was an altar server, and later a curate. It contains the remains of St. Philip Neri

An eleven-year-old Eugenio is seen here circled, with fellow members of a juvenile church circle in Rome

The newly ordained Fr. Pacelli,
Easter Sunday April 2nd, 1899

CHAPTER V

"I bless peace, not war."

On June 28th, 1914 the heir to the Imperial and Royal thrones of Austria-Hungary, Archduke Franz Ferdinand, accompanied by his morganatic wife the Duchess of Hohenberg, was paying an official visit to the Bosnian town of Sarajevo, in conjunction with Austrian troop exercises nearby. Among the cheering crowds lining the route were seven young men, all members of a Serbian terrorist group known as the Black Hand Gang; seven young men with one aim, the assassination of the Archduke. As the imperial car passed in front of three of the would-be assassins, the first two attempted to throw their grenades but were prevented from doing so by the tightly packed crowd, but a third, Cabrinovic, managed to launch his. It bounced off the hood of the car and exploded underneath the vehicle behind, injuring a number of officials. The imperial couple were unharmed, and a furious Archduke continued on his journey to the town hall. After lunch there, the plans were changed, and the couple insisted on visiting the injured at the hospital. However, on the way to the hospital the driver took a wrong turn. Realising his mistake he stopped the car and began to reverse. Another terrorist, named Gavrilo Princip, hardly able to believe his "luck," stepped forward and fired two shots. The first hit the pregnant Sophia in the stomach; she died almost instantly. The second shot hit the Archduke in the neck. He died a short while later.

That wrong turn and those fatal shots changed the course of world history, and the life of Eugenio Pacelli, for ever. The crisis that the assassination caused did not exist in a void; it came after a long series of diplomatic clashes between the Great Powers over European and colonial issues in the decade prior to 1914 which had left tensions high. Mixed with a heady brew of militarism, alliances, imperialism and nationalism, the stage was set for conflict.

Advised by Merry del Val and Pacelli, Pope Pius X was only too aware of the dangers, but his warnings to the world went unheeded. The fuse was lit, and the ensuing explosion resulted in the bloodiest war the world had ever seen. Pius' grief at the outbreak of the First World War appeared in his exhortation *Dum Europa* of August 2nd, 1914.

At the start of the war the Austro-Hungarian ambassador sought an audience of the Holy Father to ask for a papal blessing on the armies of the empire. Pius received him, flanked by Cardinal Secretary of State Merry del Val and Monsignor Pacelli. As the ambassador knelt in his presence, the aged pontiff roundly declared, "I bless peace, not war!"

Already weakened from a heart attack in 1913, it was one of his last acts. Three weeks later, on August 20th, Pope Pius X died.

As millions of men marched to war a new Pope was quickly elected. The conclave of 1914 was brief, and the need for a Pope with diplomatic skills was paramount, and on the tenth ballot the cardinals found their man. Giacomo Paolo Giovanni Battista Della Chiesa, Archbishop of Bologna, was born into the patrician classes of Genoa on November 21st, 1854. On election he took the name Benedict XV. Benedict was small in stature, earning him the nickname "piccoletto" – the little one. He was a career diplomat and had twenty years of training under Cardinals Rampolla and Merry del Val in the Vatican Foreign Office. Immediately after his election the new Pope made sweeping changes in the personnel of the Roman Curia. Merry del Val was immediately removed from the office of Secretary of State, (without, it is said, the time to even sort his papers), Cardinal Gasparri was appointed in his place, and Monsignor Pacelli moved up to Secretary of the Congregation of Extraordinary Ecclesiastical Affairs.

Benedict threw himself into his attempts to bring the war to an end and to reconcile the warring nations. His first encyclical pointed to the useless loss of so many lives, lives sacrificed on the altar of profit, business interests and territorial expansionism. The Vatican, as a neutral state, was also in an ideal position to undertake relief work for both prisoners of war and refugees, and worked tirelessly facilitating the exchange of letters between prisoners and their families. Pope Benedict gave Monsignor Pacelli responsibility for the greater part of this work. Little did he realise that the organisation he put into place during his three years in charge would be resurrected some 25 years later.

By 1916, there were faint hopes that the Central Powers – Germany and the Dual Monarchy – might be willing to consider peace talks brokered by the Vatican. President Wilson of America also made overtures, and Benedict, Gasparri and the Pacelli carefully studied the responses. During all this diplomatic manoeuvring Eugenio had his own personal sadness, when his father, Filippo, caught influenza and died on November 20th, 1916. He was 79.

The following year, the Papal Nuncio to King Ludwig III of Bavaria, Archbishop Giuseppe Aversa, died. The Bavarian nuncio was the nearest thing to an official contact with the German Kaiser that the Vatican had. His replacement would have to mix in the highest government circles, and be capable of peace negotiations on behalf of the Church herself. Pacelli was the obvious choice. His appointment was announced in April 1917, and on May 13th, amidst the splendours of the Sistine Chapel, Pope Benedict XV himself, (it would normally have fallen to Cardinal Gasparri) consecrated Eugenio as titular Archbishop of Sardes and Papal Nuncio to Bavaria.

At the conclusion of the Mass Virginia Pacelli knelt and received her son's first episcopal blessing.

Pacelli's imminent departure caused Cardinal Gasparri to declare that he felt as if his right arm had been cut off.

And on that very day in the tiny Portugese village of Fatima, three shepherd children were granted the first of their visions of the Blessed Virgin.

CHAPTER VI

"... military defeat and revolutionary chaos."

The new archbishop wasted no time in starting on his mission, leaving Rome for Bavaria on May 20th, and taking with him Pope Benedict's peace plan. He broke his journey to Munich at the Shrine of Our Lady of Einsiedeln in Switzerland.

Eugenio was under no illusions as to what awaited him in Germany, a nation exhausted by war and on the brink of revolutionary chaos.

He moved into the nuncio's official residence, a neo-classical palace on the Briennerstrasse in Munich, on May 25th. The palace was directly opposite the Brown House, later to become the infamous cradle of the Nazi Party. He presented his credentials to King Ludwig III on May 28th.

The plan itself was, out of necessity, vague on detail but contained very specific principles. When compared with President Wilson's 14-point peace plan produced many months later, the two bear striking similarities. The plan included staged disarmament, the abolition of conscription and a mechanism for arbitration in order to end hostilities. More specifically the plan proposed the restoration of all the occupied territories, with a system of arbitration for the disputed territories, such as Alsace-Lorraine, Belgium's sovereignty was to be guaranteed and Poland granted "that full and perfect liberty which is called independence."

Then, on June 28th, Archbishop Pacelli boarded the imperial train and went to see Kaiser Wilhelm II at his castle at Kreuznach, where he begged the Emperor to do all in his power to end the war. In his diary the Kaiser noted that he "liked the man from Rome well enough as a human being. But this is war. Let the British and French answer for it." Benedict XV's proposals for a peaceful settlement were off to a shaky start, though by all accounts the new nuncio did manage to persuade the Kaiser to put an end to the practice of using Belgians as slave labour in Germany, and with this one and only success the nuncio left the imperial presence for Munich to report the lack of progress to the Pope.

The problems he faced were basically insurmountable. President Wilson had tried for years to present a balanced image to the world in his handling of the warring Europeans, yet his and America's consistently pro-British stance had already led to uneven approaches even before the sinking of the Lusitania in 1915, and now with her entry into the war the Allies were confident of victory. However, Germany, buoyed by the collapse of Russia, was equally confident that it could achieve ultimate victory. Both sides jostled and vied with each other in an effort to use the Vatican to their own advantage. Pacelli learned a lesson and it wasn't one he would forget in a hurry.

In October 1917 the archbishop made a brief return to Rome to confer with Benedict and Gasparri. He arrived back in Munich under no illusion as to the future of any further Vatican peace plans. All his efforts were now turned not to statesmen and monarchs, but to the ordinary people of Germany.

When war broke out in August 1914 the British government moved immediately to strangle the supply of raw materials and foodstuffs to Germany and its allies. This marked the beginning of the 'hunger blockade,' a war of attrition that lasted until Germany signed the Treaty of Versailles in June 1919. During the final months of the war the blockade had virtually reduced the German population to a point only just above that of mass starvation.

The plight of the civil population, the refugees and the prisoners of war had an effect on the archbishop that he later likened to physical pain driving through his heart. He worked tirelessly to alleviate the misery, travelling all over Germany distributing aid and bringing what help he could. The archbishop in turn also left his own impression, and his efforts to aid the suffering of so many was remembered long after he had returned to Rome.

As Germany stumbled to defeat and starvation, another threat was beginning to manifest itself throughout the country, militant communism. Following the Russian Revolution of 1917, groups intent on fomenting revolution and anarchy began to spring up all over Germany.

The end came in November 1918. Germany sued for peace and the Kaiser fled to Holland. A republic was declared and millions of German soldiers began the painful and humiliating journey home. Their arms were intact and the belief soon took hold that the German army had not been defeated in the field, but at home, "stabbed in the back."

The end of the war saw no alleviation in the suffering of the people. The Allies refused to lift the blockade until Germany agreed to make huge reparation payments, the winter was a severe one, and then, in the summer of 1919, came the Treaty of Versailles. The new government, the Weimar Assembly, was shocked when the delegates returned with the proposals of the peace treaty: Germany was to lose some 25,000 square miles of territory, accounting for 13% of her pre-war territories. She also lost approximately six-and-a-half-million subjects, many German-speaking, and her raw material base was to be decimated. The victorious Allies gave Germany 21 days to agree the terms or else they would resume hostilities; she had no option other than to sign.

The communists were quick to exploit the bitterness and misery that resulted from defeat and the "shameful" treaty. Red flags had already begun to appear all over Germany, and by November 1918 the revolutionaries had seized all the larger coastal cities as well as Hanover, Brunswick and Frankfurt. In Munich a Workers' and Soldiers' Council forced Ludwig III to abdicate, ending over 700 years rule by the Wittelsbach dynasty, and Bavaria became the first state of the old empire to be declared a "Council Republic" (Räterepublik). In the following days the royals of all the other German states abdicated. Then on April 14th, 1919, the communists took over the

Bavarian government and declared the country a separate communist state. The world's diplomatic corps fled, either to the comparative safety of Berlin, or home – all that is, except one. Nuncio Pacelli declared that he would remain at his post. He ordered the household staff to leave for their own safety. But his German housekeeper, Sister Pasqualina, along with his secretary, valet and chauffeur all refused to leave their master.

Since the armistice Archbishop Pacelli had continued his relief work regardless of his own safety. However, the communists were fully aware of the nuncio's loathing of their atheistic creed and correctly saw him and the Church as a threat to their survival. The Nunciature was machine gunned and on one occasion was actually invaded by a mob of the Red Brigade, armed with rifles, hand grenades and revolvers. The group forced their way into the house, and demanded the papal limousine. Hurrying from his office Pacelli confronted the mob, declaring to them the extraterritoriality of the Nunciature, at which point the commander pressed a revolver against the Nuncio's chest and repeated his demand for the limousine. The mob was escorted to the garage but the chauffeur, foreseeing just such an eventuality, had disabled the vehicle. The commander then telephoned the Ministry of Military Affairs and threatened to blow up the Nunciature and that the "whole Nunciature gang,"[1] would be arrested. The car couldn't, however, be mobilised and so the mob left, and in the archbishop's own words, "all returned to peace at the Nunciature, but not for long."[1]

The communist government was a short-lived one, and in the May of 1919 the republican government's troops under General Von Epp regained control of Munich and immediately set about hunting down the communists. The former Imperial Chief of Staff, General Erich Ludendorff was put in charge and wasted no time in calling on the Nuncio to gain information on the archbishop's attackers. He must have been shocked when Pacelli refused to aid their search or take part in the persecution of his attackers. Ludendorff apparently stormed out of the meeting. Years later when the self same General Ludendorff was in danger of being tried for war crimes by an Allied court, Pacelli spoke in his defence, thus saving him from the trial.[2] What Ludendorff thought of this Christian attitude is not recorded.

1. An account of the incident by Archbishop Pacelli in the Vatican Archives
2. *Crown of Glory, The Life of Pope Pius XII*, by Alden Hatch and Seamus Walshe. Heinemann

In June 1919, a new democratic Bavarian government was proclaimed, and the threat of communism passed for the time being. However, another group was growing, cultivating like bacteria in the beer halls of Munich, equally as rabid and equally as dangerous. The Nazi Party was quick to take advantage of the belief that the German Army had been betrayed and portrayed itself as the only party that could bring Germany back to a position of superiority.

CHAPTER VII

"... the satanic spectre of Nazism."

In 1919 a third of the population of the new Germany was reckoned to be Catholic, and it had long been a wish of Pope Benedict to have a nuncio for the whole of Germany and not just Bavaria. 1919 saw negotiations with the new German government begun, largely undertaken by Pacelli, and on June 30th, 1920, Archbishop Pacelli presented his credentials to President Ebert as the first Apostolic Nuncio to a united Germany. At the same time, however, the archbishop retained the position of Nuncio to Bavaria, maintaining his palace there, and shuttling back and forth between Berlin and Munich.

On October 1st, 1921 a Bavarian newspaper, *The Bayerischer Kurier,* published what was to become a constant theme of Pacelli's time in Germany, namely a denouncement of Hitler and the Nazis. The paper quoted Nuncio Pacelli as saying "The Bavarian people are peace-loving. But just as they were seduced during the revolution by alien elements – above all Russians – into the extremes of Bolshevism, so now other non-Bavarian elements of entirely opposite persuasion have likewise thought to make Bavaria their base of operation." Of the 44 public speeches that he made on German soil before his departure in 1929, at least 40 contained attacks on National Socialism or Hitler's doctrines. He was not alone and the German bishops joined him no fewer than five times between 1920 and 1927 in making solemn pronouncements warning the faithful against National Socialism, and its racialist, anti-Christian policies.

The Nunciature in Berlin was a grand residence in a fashionable part of the city, and Pacelli launched himself into the diplomatic round with vigour and skill, his perfect manners, and well-honed diplomatic skills perfect for the new position. He hosted glittering receptions, and threw grand dinners "...which were auspicious, tastefully sprinkling glitter with the strictest European etiquette.... the nunciature was soon a major centre of Germany's social and official worlds. Streams of aristocrats, including President Paul von Hindenburg (one of Germany's Field Marshals during World War I), were frequent callers, blending with students and workers, anyone whom Pacelli, the shrewdest of diplomats, chose to smile upon."[1] Dorothy Thompson, who became the first American journalist to be expelled from Germany by Goebbels, described him at the time as "the best informed diplomat in Germany."

Retained in the archbishop's household was Sister Pasqualina, the nun who had so valiantly stood by Archbishop Paccelli during the Munich revolution. When he had first arrived in Munich, the new nuncio had called on the Prioress of the Franciscan order at Altötting, and in the course of their conversations had enquired as to the suitability of any nun to take on the role of housekeeper at the nunciature. The prioress recommended Sister Pasqualina. Pasqualina, a farmer's daughter, had been born Josefine Lehnert on August 25th, 1894, at Ebersberg in Bavaria, about 25 miles from Munich. It would seem that like the young Eugenio she was a notably pious child, turning her bedroom into a private shrine to Jesus and Our Lady, and at 15 she joined the Teaching Sisters of the Holy Cross at Altötting, near Munich, where Eugenio Pacelli was later to meet the nun who was to remain at his side for the rest of his life.

Just before the announcement of Archbishop Pacelli's appointment as Nuncio to Germany his mother, Virginia Pacelli, died on February 10th, 1920, aged 76 years. A distraught Eugenio left immediately for Rome, where he stayed until late March, when, as *The Universe* Catholic newspaper reported at the time, he returned to his post.

1. *La Popessa:* Paul I. Murphy, and R. Rene Arlington. New York 1983. Warner Books

Away from the glittering social occasions, much of Apostolic Nuncio Pacelli's time was spent setting up the relationship between the Holy See and the new German Weimar Republic. Among the difficulties he encountered, however, was that under their new constitution the German states had been declared semi-autonomous, and thus a single agreement was not possible.

The agreements that the Church worked towards were concordats, which were agreements or treaties with the force of international law between the Holy See and the government of a country, regulating relations in areas of mutual concern. This often included both recognition and privileges for the Catholic Church in a particular country. Privileges might include exemptions from certain legal matters and processes, and issues such as taxation as well as the right of a state to influence the selection of bishops within its territory. Although for a time after the Second Vatican Council, which ended in 1965, the term 'concordat' was dropped, it has since reappeared with the Polish Concordat of 1993 and the Portuguese Concordat of 2004.

The new nuncio, on behalf of the Pope, conducted all the negotiations himself, and the staunchly Catholic Bavaria was a natural place to begin. Sadly his work was interrupted on January 22nd, 1922 by the death of Pope Benedict XV. Apart from his personal grief at the loss of a friend, there was also the natural concern that a new Pope might change direction on the policies currently being pursued by the archbishop. He needn't have worried. On February 6th, 1922, an old friend Achille Ratti was elected Pope and took the name of Pius XI. Achille Ratti, Cardinal Archbishop of Milan, had spent virtually the whole of his working life as a librarian, firstly at the Ambrosian of his native Milan, and secondly at the Vatican itself. In 1919 this distinguished scholar of Medieval manuscripts and keen mountaineer was suddenly, and many thought mysteriously, taken from the Vatican Library, consecrated titular Archbishop of Lepanto, and sent as nuncio to Poland, then just emerging from Tsarist rule and where the Catholic Church was under major reconstruction. More importantly it was a nation on which communist Russia had just declared war. The Russian armies swept through Poland to the very gates of Warsaw itself.

As in Munich the diplomatic community beat a hasty retreat, but like Pacelli, Ratti stood firm and refused to flee, and his reward was to see the Polish army rout the Russians on the banks of the Vistula, forcing them off Polish soil and back to Russia. The two churchmen had much in common.

So it was with the full co-operation and backing of the new Pope that Archbishop Pacelli continued his negotiations with Bavaria. The concordat was finally signed on March 29th, 1924, and ratified by the Bavarian parliament in January 1925. It was also around this time that persistent rumours began to circulate in the national and foreign press that Archbishop Pacelli was about to be elevated to the Sacred College of Cardinals, indeed *The Universe* in Great Britain even referred to him as Cardinal Pacelli on a number of occasions. Eventually in late 1924 Archbishop Pacelli issued a categorical denial that he was about to become 'Cardinal' Pacelli.

Once the Bavarian concordat had been agreed Archbishop Pacelli moved from Munich to full-time residence in Berlin, where he immediately began work on a concordat with the most powerful of German states, Prussia. It took a further four years of negotiations and delicate diplomatic manoeuvrings before the concordat was finally signed on June 24th, 1929, being ratified on August 13th, 1929. The significance of this concordat can not be overstated, indeed such was its importance that it was considered a blueprint for the Holy See to use in its negotiations with other Protestant countries. It allowed the Catholic Church to function in a deeply Protestant state, and moreover in a country where the rising tide of Nazism and its atheistic message was beginning to make its presence and its anti-Catholic stance felt more and more.

Straight after the concordat was ratified Eugenio Pacelli allowed himself a well-earned rest in Switzerland, and it was whilst resting there that a telegram from the Holy Father arrived, announcing that he was to be elected cardinal at the next consistory and ordering him back to Rome. No rumour this time but a direct command.

By all accounts the Archbishop was saddened at the news, feeling that his work in Germany was far from over. The rise of the Nazi party, which he later called "the satanic spectre of Nazism," alarmed him and gave him further reason to wish to continue his mission in Germany. But his return was not a request but an order from the Holy Father, and it was with genuine sadness on both sides that Archbishop Pacelli began to close his nunciature. The day of his departure was an emotional one. General Paul von Hindenburg, now President of the German Republic, gave a farewell luncheon for him and all day crowds milled around his embassy, until finally, in the evening, when he stepped into an open carriage supplied by the German government for his ride to the station, a great cheer arose from the masses and an emotional archbishop gave his blessing to the people, many of whom knelt as he passed.

That the German people had deeply touched Eugenio Pacelli is beyond doubt, and he would always feel that his experience of their kindness was a true reflection of what was in their hearts, despite the future evil regime that would lure them away.

CHAPTER VIII

"To the glory of Almighty God, receive this red hat..."

Whilst Archbishop Pacelli was still at his post in Germany the papacy under its new Pope, Pius XI, took a radical turn. The Holy Father stepped onto the balcony of St. Peter's and blessed the crowd publicly instead of giving a private blessing inside, as all his predecessors had done since 1870 when Pope Pius IX had withdrawn inside the Vatican as its self proclaimed prisoner. Pope Pius IX's stance, which became known as "The Roman Question," naturally posed difficulties for dealings between the Vatican and the Kingdom of Italy.

As early as 1915 Cardinal Gasparri, in an interview approved by Benedict XV, declared that the Holy See was looking for a settlement of the Roman Question, "to the sense of justice of the Italian people." The Italian Prime Minister, Benito Mussolini, had also shown a desire for reconciliation with Pius XI. Negotiations for a settlement were finally begun in 1926, culminating in the Lateran Pacts of 1929, signed for King Victor Emmanuel III of Italy by Mussolini and for Pope Pius XI by Pietro Cardinal Gasparri.

Eugenio's brother, Francesco, like his father and family before him, had also become a lawyer and entered the service of the Holy See. He had risen rapidly, becoming dean of the lawyers of the Rota and the legal advisor to Pius XI. King Victor Emmanuel III of Italy delegated Mussolini to negotiate, and the Pope sent Gasparri and Francesco Pacelli to conduct affairs on behalf of the Vatican.

The agreements included a political treaty which created the state of Vatican City and guaranteed to the Holy See full and independent sovereignty. The Pope was pledged to perpetual neutrality in international affairs and to abstention from mediation except when specifically requested by all parties to a controversy. Also agreed on were a concordat establishing Roman Catholicism as the religion of Italy and a financial arrangement awarding money to the Holy See in settlement of all its claims against Italy arising from the loss of temporal power in 1870. The agreement was enthusiastically welcomed almost everywhere. The Italian people breathed a sigh of relief that hostilities and torn loyalties between their Pope and their King had now been removed, and a grateful Pius bestowed the title of Marquis on Francesco Pacelli.

In the December of 1929 Archbishop Pacelli arrived back in Rome. The Sacred College was to meet on December 16th, and on the evening of that day a letter was delivered to the Archbishop. Opening with his title of "Excellency," it informed him that His Holiness had been pleased to receive him into the College of Cardinals, and concluded with his new title, "Eminence." Eugenio Pacelli had been welcomed into that elite group of princes of the Church.

Three days later, on December 19th in the Sistine Chapel, he received the "Red Hat" from the hands of Pius XI, and as the Pope placed the hat upon his head pronounced, "To the glory of Almighty God, receive this red hat, a sign of the cardinal's dignity. It signifies that you should be ready to shed your blood, if necessary, in defence of the Holy Faith, and for the preservation of peace among Christians. In the name of the Father and the Son and the Holy Ghost. Amen."

Along with his red hat Cardinal Pacelli was also, as are all cardinals, appointed titular head of a church in Rome. Eugenio was appointed to the Church of Ss John and Paul, (San Giovanni e Paolo, named after the Roman Martyrs of that name, not the apostles), one of the oldest churches in a city of many ancient ones. He took possession of his church in January 1930 and in the same month the 80-year-old Cardinal Gasparri asked if he could be allowed to retire. The Holy Father acceded to his wishes. It was nearly 30 years since the then Monsignor Pietro Gasparri had knocked on the door of the young Fr. Pacelli's family home in the Via della Vetrina to recruit the young priest.

Cardinal Pacelli was his natural successor at the Secretariat of State. The Holy Father knew him both as a friend and as a diplomat, and though they were men of different temperaments, they were also men of very similar outlook. In addition they had both faced the threat of communism at first hand, the cardinal in Germany and the Pope in Poland. His appointment was announced on February 7th of that year.

The Secretariat of State, officially "Secretariat of State of His Holiness The Pope," was and is one of the chief organs of Church government. It is charged with expediting the Holy See's diplomatic affairs with civil governments, as well as many ecclesiastical affairs. It is situated in the papal palace, and its head, the Cardinal Secretary of State, is really both the Vatican's Prime Minister and Foreign Secretary. Since 1925, he also has the title of Prefect of the Sacred Congregation for Extraordinary Ecclesiastical Affairs, and so closely is he identified with the Pope and his policies that the office is vacated on the Pope's death. It must have been something akin to coming home when the new Cardinal Pacelli entered his office as Secretary of State for the first time.

Hardly had Cardinal Pacelli settled into his new office when Cardinal Merry del Val suffered an attack of appendicitis, and died on the operating table. It was a blow to Pacelli who truly mourned his old friend and mentor. Pope Pius XI appointed Eugenio to succeed Merry del Val as Archpriest of St. Peter's, adding to his duties the management of the largest Christian church in the world.

In 1924, Catholic Action (Azione Cattolica) had been established as a non-political lay organisation under the direct control of the Italian bishops. The organisation was forbidden by the Vatican to participate in politics, and had not opposed the Fascist regime, unlike the Partito Popolare. Vatican support for Catholic Action resulted in hundreds of thousands of Catholics withdrawing their former support from the Partito Popolare, and joining the apolitical Catholic Action – causing the Partito Popolare's collapse.

By article 43 of the Lateran Concordat the Italian Government had agreed to guarantee the freedom of Catholic Action to organise themselves, but since all parties but the Fascist party had been abolished by 1930, the scope for Catholic Action to operate even on a non-political basis was severely hampered, with its members even being attacked and terrorised. The Pope in response issued his famous encyclical, *Non abbiamo bisogno* (We have no need). As usual Pius XI was straightforward in his condemnation of Mussolini's actions, and didn't mince his words. What had been revealed, he said, "was the intention of monopolising the young completely from their earliest childhood till maturity, for the sole and exclusive benefit of a party, or a regime on the basis of ideology which expressly resolves itself into a veritable pagan glorification of the state ...To a Catholic such a philosophy ...is irreconcilable with Catholic doctrine and conflicts with the natural rights of the family."

However, publishing the encyclical posed a problem. The Fascists controlled the press, the radio and telecommunications; even the mail itself was being censored. If the Vatican released the encyclical in Italy, or tried to get it to a foreign country it would have been instantly suppressed or heavily censored. So Pacelli chose a young American monsignor based at the Vatican to smuggle the encyclical out of the country. He boarded a plane for Paris and literally took his life in his hands. Once in Paris he distributed the encyclical to reporters and to the world. The young priest was Monsignor Francis J. Spellman, later cardinal and Archbishop of New York, who became a lifelong friend of Cardinal Pacelli.

A furious Mussolini had no option but to discuss the issue with the Vatican, and in the September he and the cardinal signed an agreement, in which the scope of Catholic Action was defined and its freedoms guaranteed. Pacelli was a smooth operator and his consummate skills as a politician and a diplomat were coming more and more to the fore and to the attention of the world.

The problems with communicating the encyclical also taught Cardinal Pacelli an important lesson. He determined never to let himself or the Holy See get into that position again, and called upon the services of Guglielmo Marconi himself to install a radio station in Vatican City itself, by which means the Holy Father could communicate with all the world.

Archbishop Pacelli worked tirelessly to alleviate the suffering of soldiers and prisoners of war, seen here, top, with Italian soldiers and, below, German

Pictured left, This photograph from *The Universe* archives is annotated on the reverse, "Mgr Pacelli, Nuncio in Berlin, leaving the Presidential Palace, Wilhelmstrasse." It is dated January 11th, 1929. In the past copies of this photograph have been used to mislead by stating that it showed the future Pope Pius XII leaving the Presidential Palace, Berlin in March 1939. This is a deliberate attempt to suggest Pius had direct contact with Nazi officials. Hitler was, of course, not appointed Chancellor until January 1933, and Archbishop Pacelli left Germany in 1929, never to return

Cardinal Eugenio Pacelli
Papal Secretary of State

Pictured left, Beneath a canopy, Cardinal Pacelli, Papal Legate carries the Blessed Sacrament at the start of the great procession which marked the conclusion of the Budapest Congress, June 1938

Cardinal Pacelli pictured here
with Pope Pius XI

Pictured above, British Prime
Minister Neville Chamberlain
(second left) and Foreign
Secretary Viscount Halifax
(first right) visited Pope Pius
XI in January 1939, pictured
here with Cardinal Pacelli

Cardinal Pacelli visited America
in October 1936, and is seen here
at the Liberty Bell with Dennis
Cardinal Daugherty, Archbishop
of Philadelphia

CHAPTER IX

"With Burning Anxiety"

Cardinal Secretary of State Pacelli saw how the world was changing and he moved with the times. The Vatican radio station was only the start, and as the world changed and tensions mounted, Cardinal Pacelli saw that the Church must move at the same speed if it was to make its voice heard.

As America sunk into depression, it pulled Europe in its wake, and country after country began to be embroiled in financial turmoil. In Germany the economic collapse aided Hitler's Nazis, who gradually increased their grip on the country. Spain rolled headlong into bitter and bloody civil war. Mexico saw a violent left-wing government begin a systematic persecution of the Church, France teetered on the brink of anti-clerical state socialism, and another dictator, Joseph Stalin, began his reign of human misery in communist Russia.

In all these countries, and more beside, the Church and God were being relegated and persecuted. The dictators themselves were becoming Gods. There was little the Church could do in any physical sense other than support and re-assure its clergy, and to make known the universal nature of Holy Mother Church.

The days of the Pope "prisoner in the Vatican" were well and truly over. Cardinal Pacelli, for example, went as Papal Legate to the Eucharistic congress in Buenos Aires in October 1934, to the jubilee celebrations in Lourdes in April 1935, to Lisieux to dedicate the basilica of St. Therese, July 1937, and to the Eucharistic Congress at Budapest, May 1938. In

October 1936 he also travelled, in an unofficial capacity, to the United States, mainly to experience at first hand its Catholic life. Covering more than 9,000 miles by land and air he visited 12 of the 16 ecclesiastical provinces, met 79 bishops, and observed Catholicism at work in education as well as social and charitable endeavours. When he visited the Catholic university in Washington, he must have remembered, back to 1911, when the same university had offered him the post of Professor of Roman Law.

In all he did to formulate and propagate Vatican policy during this period Cardinal Pacelli and Pope Pius were as one, and no evidence has ever come to light of even the slightest variance on policy. Indeed the Holy Father once stated, "Cardinal Pacelli speaks with my voice." Yet never were two men more different in character and temperament, as the following description sums up nicely: "Achille Ratti was small, and heavy; slow in his movements, with a hard will. He was like a dormant volcano: slow to erupt, but capable of violent bursts of energy. Pacelli was tall and slim, as quick and versatile as a chameleon, and as lively as the dancing blue flame of a turf fire. But their opposite qualities produced apposition between them. They supplemented each other. And they were true friends." [1]

During this time Cardinal Pacelli was also responsible for drawing up concordats with Austria, Yugoslavia and other nations, with the aim of regulating relations in areas of mutual concern, regarding the Catholic Church and the country in question.

On gaining power in Germany some Nazis declared (although not Hitler) that the concordats previously agreed upon with the individual German states were no longer valid. However, at Easter 1933, the regime proposed exploring a new concordat with the Holy See. It is worth noting here that previously, (March 24th), the Centre party and the Bavarian People's Party, whom German Catholics rightly considered representatives of their interests, had approved the enabling act that gave Hitler unlimited powers. Also the German bishops had declared unequivocally that Catholics could co-operate with the new state despite obviously irreconcilable differences between the Catholic Church and National Socialism (March 28th).

1. *Crown of Glory, The Life of Pope Pius XII,* by Alden Hatch and Seamus Walshe. Heinemann

Cardinal Pacelli had in no way influenced any of these events; yet he had to take them into consideration. Critics of Cardinal Pacelli and of the concordat usually point to article 16 of the treaty, which required bishops, before taking possession of their diocese, to take an oath of fealty to the State concerned or to the President of the Reich. But for a perfect assessment of the article in question we can do no better than turn to Monsignor Ronald Knox, who succinctly points out that in so doing the Pope and Cardinal Pacelli did not intend, "anything more than recognition of the German government as the constituted government of the country."[2] It takes a long stretch of the imagination to construe this as meaning the Church's total acceptance of all the government's ideas, policies and actions.

The new concordat also agreed to all the demands of the Holy See, even to the continuation of Catholic schools, and the earlier concordats with the German states. The Holy See could not fulfil its duty to protect the Catholics of Germany by any means other than negotiation and treaty with Berlin. Here at least was a legal basis on which the Holy See could mount a protest in defence of the Catholic population.

Article 32 stated that the Church was not to take part in politics, and it has often been said that this led to the disintegration of Germany's Centre Party. This is very far from the truth, for what the terms stated was that the clergy and religious were to take no part in party politics, but they were most certainly not restricted, and nor did they consider themselves to be restricted in commenting and condemning infringements of human rights. Catholic lay people were free to take part in whatever politics they wished as long as their actions were compatible to God's law. The Centre Party itself collapsed before the concordat was even signed.

One very important part of the concordat was that the German government agreed that when Jewish people converted from Judaism to Christianity, that they would regard them henceforth as Christians and no longer Jewish. This latter clause would provide thousands of Jews with an escape route from the deportation orders via the Catholic Church, which issued them with baptismal certificates, whether or not they had been baptised.

2. *Nazi and Nazarene*, R.Knox, Macmillan

Pope Pius went so far as to state that he had only signed the agreement "despite many and grave misgivings." He was, of course, made fully aware through the warnings of his Secretary of State that Hitler and his regime were most unlikely to keep to the terms. Pacelli also made it clear to Sir Ivone Kirkpatrick, a Catholic, and the chargé d'affaires of the British Legation to the Vatican, that the choice he was faced with was a stark one, a concordat that offered huge concessions that were unlikely to be met, or the virtual elimination of the Church in Germany. [3]

As both the Pope and the cardinal had suspected it didn't take the Nazis long to start violating the concordat. Catholic youth groups were closed down, as were Catholic newspapers and printing companies. As the persecutions grew so did the protests from the Church and from local clergy. As a result the Nazis arrested clergymen in ever increasing-numbers on trumped-up charges that ranged from immorality to currency violations.

The Vatican itself began to formally protest about the actions of the Nazis almost immediately after the concordat was signed. The first formal Catholic protests under the concordat concerned the Nazi government's call for a boycott of Jewish businesses, and its sterilisation laws, which ordered the compulsory sterilisation of all Germans with physical or mental impairments. Numerous protests would follow over the treatment of both the Jews and the direct persecution of the Church in Nazi Germany. The German foreign minister would report that his desk was "stuffed with protests from Rome." Between 1933 and 1939 there were no fewer than 60 protests by Cardinal Pacelli to Hitler's government, all written in the cardinal's hand and all testimony to his struggle to have the German government observe the concordat.

By 1937 the German bishops were exasperated at the lack of any response by the Hitler government to their protests. A deputation was despatched to Rome to meet with Cardinal Secretary of State Pacelli. Prior to their arrival the cardinal had already begun to make notes on a possible reaction to the situation, and these he passed onto Cardinal Faulhaber of the deputation, whom he asked to develop them into the basis of a papal encyclical.

3. *The Inner Circle – Memoirs of Ivone Kirkpatrick*, Macmillan

The decision was also taken to publish the encyclical in German. The initial drafts condemning Nazi ideology were then developed by Pacelli into a powerful denunciation of the anti-semitic Nazi creed of Fascism and racialism. In it he said, "Whoever exalts race, or the people, or the state, or a particular form of state, or the depositaries of power, or any other fundamental value of the human community – however necessary and honourable be their function in worldly things – whoever raises these notions above their standard values and divinises them to an idolatrous level, distorts and perverts an order of the world planned and created by God; he is far from the true faith in God, and from the concept of life which that faith upholds." He went on, "none but superficial minds could stumble into concepts of a national God, of a national religion; or attempt to lock within the frontiers of a single people, within the narrow limits of a single race, God the Creator of the universe, King and Legislator of all nations, before whose immensity they are 'as a drop of water in a bucket.'" He also amended Faulhaber's original title for the encyclical from "With Great Anxiety" to "With Burning Anxiety" *(Mit brennender Sorge).*

Cardinal Pacelli knew that once an inkling of the encyclical's contents became known in Germany, then it would never make it over the frontier. Thus it was not only published in German, but was actually printed in Germany. Individual towns and villages received and printed it clandestinely, passing it on through teams of motorcyclists to avoid the public mail system. It arrived in all the great cathedrals, and the tiniest parish churches, on the Saturday evening or early hours of Sunday morning – Palm Sunday – all in time to be read aloud at Sunday morning Mass. In many of the great German cathedrals the bishops' themselves read it aloud.

The Nazis were furious and their reaction was swift. Copies were seized, distributors arrested, and any publications that reproduced it were banned. There also followed a wave of arrests and trials of clergy, grants to Catholic theology students were withdrawn and a slanderous media campaign begun.

Cardinal Pacelli wrote an open letter to Cardinal Schulte, Archbishop of Cologne, calling on the hierarchy and clergy of Germany to fight the evil of Nazism, "When the Holy Church, and the Supreme Pontiff are made the targets of outrageous attacks, when the lying attempt is made to trump up an antagonism between loyalty to the Church and loyalty to the earthly fatherland, then the hour is struck when the bishop must raise his voice and fearlessly repeat the words of the Apostle, 'Whether it be right to harken unto you, more than to God.'"

CHAPTER X

"Scatter the nations which desire wars"

During these turbulent times, crisis seemed to follow crisis. In 1935 Mussolini, who had long craved a new Italian Empire based on that of the Ancient Romans, decided to launch his bid for "a place in the sun." He began his quest for empire by invading Abyssinia and avenging the Italian defeat of March 1896, at the Battle of Adowa.

Pacelli and the Pope were horrified and the Italian people were whipped up to a frenzy by the state-controlled media. The Lateran Pact prevented the Pope from direct interference in Italian politics. It did not, however, prevent him from speaking his mind. Yet in an ominous portent for the future, Pius XI was accused of not doing enough to prevent the war, and of an "ominous silence."[1] It is said that the British Foreign Secretary at the time noted, "The Pope appears to be so timid as to give the impression that he supports Mussolini," and it has been written that the Vatican "played its usual card of political neutrality, offering merely bland utterances..."

Pius addressed his cardinals in Rome on the subject: "Since universal rumours of war are spread abroad and cause the greatest fear and agitation everywhere, we consider it opportune, in virtue of the apostolic office entrusted to us, to speak our mind. That peoples should once more take to arms against each other, that brethren should again shed each

1. *The Catholic Church and Reason*, Radio talk given by Rev. Henry Johnston, S.J, 1956

other's blood, that from earth, sea and sky should come ruin and destruction, this is a crime so enormous, a manifestation of such mad folly, that we hold it to be absolutely impossible, according to the judicial saying, 'What is against justice is not to be considered a possibility.'

"We cannot be persuaded that those who should have at heart the prosperity and well-being of the peoples are ready for the ruin and extermination not only of their own nation, but of a great part of humanity. But if anyone thinks of committing this infamous crime – may God put far off the realisation of such a sorrowful presage, which on our part we believe unthinkable – then we can only again direct to God with anguished soul the prayer *'Dissipa gentes quae bella volunt.'* Scatter the nations which desire wars."

This then is "ominous silence?" It is truly remarkable that people who previously never listened to a word or suggestion uttered by the Holy Father were suddenly smitten with a desire for his guidance and leadership. They then closed their ears to his words and complained that he had not spoken.

History was now repeating itself and in the same way that during the First World War Benedict XV made several attempts to bring about peace – indeed would have saved the world from the worst consequences of the war and of the peace that followed had he been listened to. Pius was now blamed for not trying to bring about peace. In the years to come the future Pius XII would be accused along similar lines.

In the middle of all the turbulence, in April 1935, Francesco Pacelli died. Shortly afterwards Cardinal Pacelli travelled to the shrine at Lourdes for the jubilee celebrations, and it is not difficult to imagine the sorrow he felt following the loss of his elder brother.

Whilst at Lourdes Cardinal Pacelli, assisted by Cardinal van Roey and Luigi Maglione, the Apostolic Nuncio to Paris, celebrated pontifical Mass. He preached on the modern pagan ideas of racialism and totalitarianism, ending with the words "...It matters little that they mass around the flag of social revolution. They are inspired by a false conception of the world and life. Whether they are possessed by superstitions of race and blood or by false conceptions of the social and economic world, their philosophy is essentially opposed to the Christian faith. And on such principles the Church does not consent to form a compact with them at any price."

More dramatic events were to follow. In March 1938 Hitler marched into Austria and declared the Anschluss, or union of Austria with Germany. There now began an instant persecution of the Catholic Church. Priests were arrested, offices of Catholic Action closed, Catholic Women's organisations were disbanded, all Catholics holding senior posts at the university of Salzburg were dismissed, and overnight the Catholic press became totally Nazi controlled. However, the Catholic Archbishop of Vienna, Theodor Innitzer, arranged for his cathedral bells to be rung in welcome for the Nazis, and for some of his churches to be festooned with swastika flags. He then compounded this lunacy by urging Austrians to vote in the plebiscite for the Anschluss.

Vatican Radio immediately broadcast a vehement denunciation of his suggestion, and Pacelli ordered the erring prelate to Rome forthwith. He was subsequently made to sign a statement on his own behalf and on behalf of the whole Austrian Episcopate. The statement said unequivocally that his former declarations should in no way be understood as an approval of what was not compatible with God's law, and the freedom and rights of the Catholic Church.

The following month Hitler paid a visit to Rome at Mussolini's invitation. Before he arrived the Pope and Cardinal Pacelli left for Castel Gandolfo in order to express their disapproval, and when Hitler expressed an interest in seeing the Vatican Museums, it was announced that they had been "closed for repairs."

At the end of the same month Pope Pius sent his Cardinal Secretary to Hungary to attend the International Eucharistic Congress in Budapest. He used all his energies whilst there to warn the world of the impending disaster which would result from either active participation with the forces of evil or even in doing nothing and being "swept along" on its tide.

Then in July Mussolini, urged on by Hitler, passed laws that restricted the civil rights of Italian Jews. Italy had only a small Jewish population, and little history of anti-semitism. The Italians, being Italians, chose to ignore the new laws or found ways and means to flout them, or even sabotage them. Pope Pius reacted angrily against the so-called "Aryan manifesto," calling it "a true form of apostasy," and that "the spirit of faith must fight against the spirit of separatism, and of exaggerated nationalism which are detestable and which, just because they are not Christian, end by not being even human."[4]

In September 1938 while negotiations took place between the main powers an even greater crisis struck, this time over Czechoslovakia. Hitler demanded that the Sudetenland be ceded to Germany. For two weeks the world held its collective breath until, in the September, came the infamous Munich accord, signed by Neville Chamberlain for Britain, Edouard Daladier for France, Mussolini for Italy and Adolf Hitler for Germany. Hitler promised that if he were given the Sudetenland he would ask for nothing more and that his territorial ambitions would be at an end. The Sudetenland was thrown to the wolves.

In the January of 1939, Neville Chamberlain and his Foreign Secretary, Lord Halifax, were received in private audience by the Pope. They also had a long conference with Cardinal Pacelli, but the world continued its slow drift to war.

February 11th would see the tenth anniversary of the Lateran Treaty, and celebrations were also planned in St. Peter's to coincide with the sixtieth anniversary of the Pope as a priest.

Then, on February 9th, the Holy Father suffered a heart attack. The doctors pronounced it only slight, made Pius comfortable for the night, and Eugenio retired to his rooms. Unable to sleep, however, he was awake and dressed when in the early hours of February 10th there came a knock at his door and a Vatican official informed him that the Holy Father's health had deteriorated dramatically. He went straight to the Papal apartment where he knelt at his friend's bedside. The end was swift and at 5.30 am Pope Pius XI died peacefully in his bed. A clearly distraught Eugenio bent over his friend's body and gently kissed his forehead.

4. *Pius XII*, Ethel Tolansky and Helena Scott, CTS

CHAPTER XI

"Miserere Mei"

Pacelli had been appointed Camerlengo of the Church by Pope Pius XI in 1935, which meant that on the death of the Holy Father he was the one who must make all the decisions until a Conclave met and a new Pope was elected.

In the three weeks following Pius' death Rome was abuzz with gossip and speculation, all played out against a backdrop of mounting world tension and the threat of world war. 62 cardinals were eligible to vote: 35 Italians and 27 non-Italians. As Camerlengo and ex Secretary of State* Eugenio Pacelli was by far the most powerful of them all, and whether this would be an advantage or a disadvantage to his chances of being elected Pope was the subject of much speculation as the Conclave began on March 1st, 1939.

Voting started the following day and on only the second ballot Eugenio Pacelli was elected Pope. It was his 63rd birthday. Cardinal Caccia-Dominioni, the Senior Cardinal Deacon, asked of Eugenio, "Accipisne electionem?" "Accipio" he replied, and as the cardinals cheered and he took off his cardinal's robes to be dressed in the papal cassock, he repeated again and again, "Miserere Mei" – have pity on me. It had been the shortest conclave for 300 years.

Eugenio would have been familiar with the Pacelli family story of Monsignor Jacobacci's prophecy at his baptism: "Sixty-three years from today the people in St. Peter's and all Rome will loudly praise this child."

In honour of Achilli Ratti he took the name Pius XII. Naming March 12th as the day of his coronation, he further decided that it would be

---

* At the death of a Pope the Secretary of State loses his office.

performed in public. His immediate predecessors, Leo XIII and Benedict XV, had been crowned in the privacy of the Sistine Chapel, and Pius XI's coronation, though semi-public, had been a modest affair. This time the Mass would be said inside St. Peter's but with the crowning taking place on the balcony in full view of the 70,000 spectators in the square. The floor of the balcony was to be raised to the height of the parapet, making a stage that all could see. In fact the whole world would see and hear, for the event was, for the first time, to be filmed from start to finish as well as broadcast on the wireless.

Missing from the 40,000 ticket holders in the basilica were any senior representatives from Nazi Germany, (who only sent their Vatican ambassador) and from Communist Russia. A clear snub to the new Pope and a clear message that Pius was firmly regarded by the Axis powers as anti-Nazi. The official SS journal, *Das Schwarze Korps*, carried the following assessment of the new Pope: "As Papal Nuncio, and Vatican Secretary of State, Pacelli showed little understanding of our position: we have low expectations of him; we don't expect him to change his ways as Pope."

The new Pope was all too aware of the critical world situation. During the six months between his election and the outbreak of war on September 1st he did all in his power to prevent its outbreak. He put in place a team to help. Cardinal Maglione was appointed as his Secretary of State, with Monsignor Tardini as head of the Vatican Office of Extraordinary Ecclesiastical Affairs, with Monsignor Montini (later Pope Paul VI) as Head of the Office of Ordinary Ecclesiastical Affairs.

On August 24th he broadcast to the world, pleading for peace and for nations to step back from the brink of war. During this speech he uttered the famous phrase, "Nothing is lost with peace: everything may be lost with war." He also attempted, to no avail, to get five of the countries principally involved to a peace conference, but on September 1st Germany invaded Poland from the west, followed shortly by its new ally Russia invading from the east. On the third of that month, in keeping with their pact with Poland, Britain and France declared war on Germany. The Second World War had begun.

In October 1939 the new Pope issued his first encyclical, *Summi Pontificatus*. At the time of writing Pius must have remembered the criticism that had been levelled at Benedict XV during the First World War, when he was criticised for refusing to pass moral judgement on unjust aggression by countries. The same criticism cannot be levelled at *Summi Pontificatus*, which, whilst not explicit, is crystal clear in its condemnation of the religious, racial and political policies of both Nazi Germany and Communist Russia.

With the invasion of Poland Pius soon learned of the horrors of modern war, and had a taste of the criticisms for his actions that were soon to persist. People immediately began to urge him to speak out and condemn the Nazi and Communist atrocities. The exiled Polish bishops told him the people felt abandoned, the Allies urged him on. But Pius was also listening to another point of view contrary to the exiled bishops. Many Polish bishops inside the beleaguered nation began to beg the Holy Father not to speak publicly, as they feared that each time he did so matters would be made worse. Pius concluded that quiet diplomacy was the best way to resolve problems. Linked to this was the fact that secure communication with his clergy was impossible after 1940 when the Germans forbade Polish clergy from leaving the country.

It is worth examining here the view that stronger protests, not just over Poland but throughout the war, would have made matters worse. Hard, fast and consistent evidence to support this argument is really difficult to come by. The main stumbling block is that there was never any consistency in German reprisals. For example, in Holland, the protests of bishops in a pastoral letter read in all churches led directly to the killing or deportation of Jews who had converted to Catholicism. In France, however, when the bishops protested at the deportation of the Jews, no reprisals were taken against Jewish Catholic converts – although they were not to escape the attentions of the Nazis forever.

It is also hard to believe that Hitler, so intent on the destruction of the Jews that he was willing to risk the German war effort to achieve it, would really have taken notice of Papal threats at any time during the war. Should Pius have gone in for the great theatrical gestures, such as that of

Bishop Felice Roeder of Beauvais who, when the Vichy government issued an edict calling upon all Jews to register with the authorities, claimed Jewish ancestry and showed up at the Town Hall in full vestments, preceded by an acolyte carrying a crucifix?[1]

For Pius to have emulated any of these gestures would have been a total and shattering break not only with his own reserved personality but also with a lifetime's training in the Vatican Diplomatic Service.

Perhaps grand gestures were contemplated. On February 11th, 1983, *The Universe Catholic Weekly* carried a story on its front page revealing that Pius had personally burned, page by page, a condemnation he had written concerning Nazi brutality in Holland. This was revealed by Sr. Pasqualina, then 89, who stated that she clearly recalled the episode.

When the Dutch bishops in a pastoral letter condemned the Nazi deportations in Holland, and in retaliation the Nazis rounded up it was said, some 40,000 people,* Pius wrote four pages of outraged condemnation. Suddenly he had second thoughts. He went into the kitchen of his apartment, lit a stove and destroyed the pages one by one, burning his hand in his agitation. He explained to his housekeeper; "I wrote this protest so that it could be published in this afternoon's *L'Osservatore Romano*. "Then I thought that if 40,000 innocent people were sent to concentration camps after what the bishops wrote, then for what the Pope has written Hitler could intern at least 200,000 people. I cannot allow it." In an interesting aside she also informed *Universe* readers that Pius' working day lasted from 6.15 am until 2.00 am the next day.

His own statements also confirm that Pius weighed his words and his actions with the greatest care, always fearful of what might result from them. In addressing the Sacred College on June 2nd, 1942, he said, "Every word that we addressed to the responsible authorities and every one of Our public declarations had to be seriously pondered and considered, in the interests of the persecuted themselves, so as not, unwittingly, to make the situation still harder and more intolerable."

In writing to Bishop von Preysing of Berlin in 1943, the Pope confided: "...We must leave to the local Church authorities to judge how far, and in what degree, in the events of Episcopal declarations, the danger of

1. *The Tablet*, October 24th, 1942, sadly though there is no independent confirmation of this incident

* The figure of 40,000 is mentioned by some newspapers but without foundation in fact. Pius XII did not know that the figure was pure speculation and had no means of verifying it.

reprisals and pressures, as well perhaps as other conditions brought about by the duration and psychology of the war, it may be advisable to practise restraint *ad maiora mala vitanda*... for the Vicar of Christ the path We must tread, to find the right balance between the conflicting demands of his pastoral office, is ever more tortuous and strewn with thorns."

It is thus impossible to say what the effects throughout the war of different papal protests or gestures would have been. What is certain, however, is that there is not a scrap of real evidence to suggest that Pope Pius XII had anything other than the most noble motives in all he did as he strove to protect innocent lives. A different Pope might have done otherwise and made rash pronouncements – and the effects could have been catastrophic.

The newly crowned Pope wears the triple crown after his public coronation on Sunday, March 12th, 1939

A striking study of the Holy Father addressing ecclesiastical colleges and seminaries in the Court of St. Damaso on June 30th, 1939, prior to the outbreak of war

Despite the Pope's best efforts Rome was bombed, causing over 1,000 deaths and 6,000 wounded. Immediately after the raid on July 19th, 1943, Pius XII, along with Mgr. Montini travelled to the Basilica di San Lorenzo fuori le Mura which had been badly damaged. There he prayed with his people and distributed Vatican funds to enable those who had lost everything to at least buy food and find shelter

Sister Pasqualina Lehnert

Pictured above, Catholic industrialist Myron C. Taylor and his wife Anabel at the Vatican in June 1941. With them is Bishop Joseph Hurley of St. Augustine, Florida, the first American to become a nuncio for the Vatican

The Holy Father is borne from the Sistine Chapel on the seventh anniversary of his coronation in March 1946

CHAPTER XII

... and the maelstrom swirled about his head

Once the war had begun one of Pius' major aims was to try and keep Italy out of the war. He was assisted in this aim by United States' President Franklin D. Roosevelt, who had similar designs. The United States, however, had no direct contact with the Holy See and there had not been any diplomatic relations between the two since 1868. The Americans at this stage were not mindful to establish any either, so the President suggested to Monsignor Amleto Cicognani, the Apostolic Delegate in Washington, that he send a personal envoy to the Holy Father instead. The Pope liked the idea, and Roosevelt appointed the American industrialist and philanthropist Myron C. Taylor to the post.

Taylor's appointment was announced on December 23rd, 1939, and confirmed in Rome on February 28th, 1940. He was to serve throughout the rest of Roosevelt's presidency (he died in 1945) and continued as President Harry S. Truman's personal envoy until 1950. At roughly the same time the Pope also received the new Italian ambassador to the Vatican, Dino Alfieri, and expressed to the new ambassador his confidence that his concerns on behalf of peace and justice would always find an echo, "in the courageous, strong and hard-working Italian people, whose wise leaders and their own inner feelings have till now happily preserved them from the danger of being implicated in the war."[1]

---

1. *Pius XII and the Second World War, According to the Archives of the Vatican*, Pierre Blet, S.J. Gracewing

Two weeks later he received at the Vatican the King and Queen of Italy, Victor Emmanuel III and Queen Elena. Once again Pius praised Italy's love of peace... "under the majestic and wise hand of its emperor-king, and through the clear sighted direction of its rulers..."

Then, throwing protocol to the wind for once, Pius XII decided to visit the Italian sovereigns in person, and on December 28th he entered the former palace of the Popes, the Quirinal, which had been the residence of the kings of Italy since 1870. Once again his pleas for peace were to the fore.

Mussolini had not been present at the meeting between his sovereign and the Holy Father, and was unnerved. The Pope's repeated appeals for Italian neutrality were not, he knew, the sort of talk to appeal to the Führer. Furthermore the great Duce, who had spoken so grandiloquently of the glories of war for almost two decades, had suddenly got cold feet now the war had broken out – even going so far as to invent a new description for Italy's status when he deemed 'neutrality' to be an insufficiently Fascist term: Italy was now a 'non-belligerency.'

On January 5th, 1940 Mussolini wrote what he hoped was a reassuring letter to Hitler: "The recent exchange of visits between the King and the Pope were primarily of an internal, not international, nature. The conversations were brief and general without producing any decision or proposals, and it could not have been otherwise." [1]

He then went on to inform Hitler of his own concerns about Italy entering into combat on the side of the Germans, going so far as to suggest a reconstituted independent Polish state in order to ameliorate the Allies and end the war. He even had the temerity to opine, "But it is not certain that the Allies can be brought to their knees or even divided. To believe so is to delude oneself. The United States will not allow the democracies to be completely defeated." He was right. Hitler did not like it.

In April 1940 Hitler's legions invaded Denmark and Norway. On March 24th Pius again wrote to Mussolini and begged him to remain neutral. He was joined in his pleas by President Roosevelt who sent no fewer than three messages to the Italian dictator warning him to stay clear of the war. On May 10th Hitler unleashed his Panzers and the Luftwaffe against the Low Countries, with devastating results. The centre of Rotterdam was

1. *Pius XII and the Second World War, According to the Archives of the Vatican*, Pierre Blet, S.J. Gracewing

destroyed in under twenty minutes, and the triumphant Panzers swept on into France.

A clearly shaken Pius sent moving telegrams of condolence to the royal sovereigns of Belgium, Holland and Luxembourg, promising to pray for them. To the Protestant Queen Wilhelmina of Holland he wrote, "We beg God the Supreme Ruler of mankind that, as quickly as possible, He may restore justice and liberty."[1]

By June 10th the Nazis were at the gates of Paris, and it was only then that Mussolini, nervous about being left out of the spoils in a Hitler-dominated Europe, brought Italy into the war. Italian armies were sent scuttling over the Alpine passes, and on the same day President Roosevelt said, "The hand that held a dagger has stuck it into the back of his neighbour."[2] The parade of disasters that followed still boggles the mind: Savoy, Sidi Barrani, Taranto, Greece, Beda Fomm.

As the world descended into chaos, and the maelstrom swirled about his head, Pius still remembered the Vatican's responsibility and its ability to provide relief work. He immediately set in motion relief projects, using the systems he had devised during the First World War. The Pontifical Relief Commission soon had agencies throughout Europe. Their main function was to organise the purchase and distribution of supplies of food and clothing, mainly from the United States.

Again drawing on his experiences during the First War, Pius set up an organisation for the facilitating of correspondence between prisoners of war and their families. The bureau, based in the Palazzo San Carlo, was open to anyone (including those of any religion or none) to contact. Its primary purpose was to locate members of families who had been deported, imprisoned, were missing in action or who had simply disappeared. The bureau was an amazing organisation, meticulously noting every letter and item that arrived, forwarding the information where possible, if not filing it and saving it for future matching and forwarding. During the whole of the war and its aftermath over nine million messages were processed, and thousands upon thousands of people were successfully located.

The work must have been as heart-rending as it was rewarding. "I am not a Catholic," wrote an Australian mother, "but I am certain that you

1. *Pius XII and the Second World War, According to the Archives of the Vatican*, Pierre Blet, S.J. Gracewing
2. *Crown of Glory, The Life of Pope Pius XII*, by Alden Hatch and Seamus Walshe. Heinemann

who are so good will endeavour to help me find my son." A prisoner anxious about his aged mother who was ill asked for news as soon as possible ...but how could he obtain information about her while confined in Johannesburg and thousands of miles separated them? Only the Pope could bridge the distance... and he did, around 10 days later, when Vatican officials gave the prisoner the re-assurance he was seeking, that his mother was fine.[3]

It was said that if it were for this work alone, Pius XII deserved a monument.

3. *Pope Pius XII Architect for Peace*, Margherita Marchione, Paulist Press

"a lonely voice"

Pius had seen the importance and understood the wide-ranging uses of the radio as early as 1930, and by 1931 had set up the Vatican Radio station with the assistance of Marconi himself. And now that medium came into its own as never before. Throughout the whole of the war the Pope's and the Vatican's messages were broadcast around the world, without a doubt bringing hope and strength to many. But they were also controversial and mired in dispute. Berlin called for prudence, and lodged complaints, and the Allies protested against the Pope's reserve. The same old arguments going around and around, with both sides criticising the Pope.

It was not only the warring nations who could disagree. The Church herself found no general consensus as to the advantage or otherwise of Vatican Radio. For example, the auxiliary Bishop of Kaunas in Lithuania, which was under Soviet occupation, wrote that the broadcasts in his own language which were directed against the Bolsheviks had no effect other than to rile up the Soviet authorities against the Church. He went on to make the very valid point that everyday life itself under the Russian heel was antidote enough against the horrors of communism.[1]

To add further to the problems, broadcasts themselves were frequently circulated out of context, with extracts taken from them and serious inexactitudes added. Pius knew, however, that it was his Christmas messages that would be the most widely listened to, and his Christmas message of 1942 is generally regarded as the most important, far-ranging

1. *Pius XII and the Second World War, According to the Archives of the Vatican,* Pierre Blet, S.J. Gracewing

and forthright of them all. In it he specifically denounced the extermination of the Jews, and spoke strongly of, "the hundreds of thousands who through no fault of their own, and solely because of their nation or race, have been condemned to death or progressive extinction." By anyone's standards the strong message behind these words could not have been clearer.

It prompted the *The New York Times* to praise the message, writing, "This Christmas more than ever Pope Pius XII is a lonely voice crying out in the silence of a continent. The pulpit whence he speaks is more than ever like the Rock on which the Church was founded, a tiny island lashed and surrounded by a sea of war... When a leader bound impartially to nations on both sides condemns as heresy the new form of national state which subordinates everything to itself; when he declares that whoever wants peace must protect against 'arbitrary attacks' the 'juridical safety of individuals;' when he assails violent occupation of territory, the exile and persecution of human beings for no reason other than race or political opinion; when he says that people must fight for a just and decent peace, a 'total peace' – the 'impartial' judgment is like a verdict in our high court of justice."

Lest it be thought the Nazis had missed the point we need look no further than Reinhard Heydrich's *Reich Main Security Office (RSHA)* which, referring to the broadcast, published the following on January 22nd, 1943: "In a manner never known before the Pope has repudiated the National Socialist New Order ...his speech is one long attack on everything we stand for ...God, he says, regards all peoples and races as worthy of the same consideration. Here he is clearly speaking on behalf of the Jews ...he is virtually accusing the German people of injustice towards the Jews, and makes himself the mouthpiece of the Jewish war criminals." [2]

On July 10th, 1943, the Allies began their invasion of Axis-controlled Europe when they landed on Sicily. They encountered little resistance from the demoralised Italian troops, and within three days, 150,000 Allied troops were ashore.

Mussolini by this point had become nothing more than Hitler's puppet, and his grand vision of turning a Fascist Italy into a new Roman Empire lay in tatters. By the spring of 1943, opposition groups within Italy were

2. *The Cross and the Third Reich,* John Frain, Family Publications

beginning to unite in an effort to overthrow him and make peace with the Allies.

In Rome itself the invasion had led prominent members of the Italian Fascist government to turn against Mussolini. Among them were his *confidant,* Dino Grandi, and Mussolini's son-in-law, Count Galeazzo Ciano. With several of his colleagues close to revolt, il Duce was forced to summon the Grand Council of Fascism, the first time that body had met since the start of the war. Grandi moved a resolution asking the King to resume his full constitutional powers – in effect, a vote of no confidence in Mussolini. The motion carried by a 19-7 margin. Despite this Mussolini arrived at his office the next day as usual. He allegedly viewed the Grand Council as merely an advisory body and did not think the vote would have any substantive effect. But that afternoon King Victor Emmanuel made his move and summoned Mussolini to the royal palace. When Mussolini tried to tell the King about the meeting, Victor Emmanuel cut him off and told him that Marshal Pietro Badoglio was replacing him. On leaving the palace, he was arrested by Carabinieri on the King's orders.

Mussolini was arrested in the July and by early September the Germans had occupied northern and central Italy and finally on September 10th, 1943 they occupied Rome itself. At this time there were approximately 12,000 Jews living in the city. The Gestapo wasted no time. Aided by the Jewish registration lists created in the days when Mussolini and his Fascist government had issued anti-Jewish decrees, Gestapo officers began to organise their deportation.

In late September Colonel Herbert Kappler, the SS commander in Rome, ordered the Jewish community to hand over 50 kilograms of gold within 36 hours or else he would deport 200 hostages to the concentration camps. The Jewish writer Pinchas E Lapide commented: "As soon as the Vatican found out about this, it discreetly informed the leaders of the Jewish community that, if the required quantity of gold could not be collected within the stipulated time, it would furnish whatever was missing." Lapide then quotes Professor Oscar Halecki who said: "Pius XII instructed the Vatican treasurer to raise whatever gold was still required, although it turned out that Vatican help was not needed after all.

The Nazis of course had no intention of honouring the bargain and a horrified Pius learned on the morning of October 16th that a Nazi raid the night before had taken over 1,000 Jews, transporting them away in trucks. Pius issued urgent instructions that all convents, church buildings and monasteries were to be opened to Jewish refugees. It has been estimated that by the end of October as many as one-third of the Jewish population of Rome were in hiding in buildings owned by the Catholic Church. Pope Pius himself hid some 1,500 Jewish refugees in his summer residence at Castel Gandolfo. On the Pope's behalf Cardinal Maglione summoned Baron Ernst von Weizsäcker, the German ambassador. The ambassador voiced his sympathies and regrets, going so far as to say he was ashamed and appalled by his leader's actions, but when he was pressed to relay a protest to his government from the Vatican and a request for a halt to the Jewish arrests, asked that the Vatican allow him to handle the situation personally.

This move was consistent with von Weizsäcker's actions throughout his time as ambassador to the Holy See. He always attempted to protect the Holy Father and to represent his views in the most favourable light he could, thus hoping to persuade his masters that the Vatican was in fact sympathetic to the Germans, while at the same time doing as little as possible to avoid irritating the Nazis. To achieve his aims he usually therefore preferred to make his own representations of the views of the Holy See. Weizsäcker also became convinced, probably with good reason, that the Nazis intended to kidnap Pius before the Allies reached Rome, and therefore he sent what his lieutenant Albrecht von Kessel later called "tactical lies" to protect the Pope by persuading the Nazis that Pius would not do anything to injure the German cause.

On the occasion of the Maglione interview on the morning after the raids, Weizsäcker sent his now infamous telegram to Berlin which has done so much to injure the reputation of Pius XII, but which can be interpreted very differently when read in the light of the Baron's private attitude towards Berlin and the Holy See. The telegram read:

"The Curia is particularly shocked that the action took place, so to speak, under the Pope's window. The reaction would be perhaps softened if the

Jews could be used for military work in Italy. The groups in Rome hostile to us exploit the action to force the Vatican out of its reserve. They say that in French towns where similar things happened, bishops took a clear position, and the Pope, as head of the Church, could not do less. People are beginning to contrast this Pope with his much more fiery predecessor, Pius XI. Enemy propaganda abroad will certainly seize the occasion to provoke tensions between the Curia and ourselves."[3] [Weizsäcker's communique to Berlin suggests that the Pope was merely upset by the rounding up of the Jews as it appeared to lessen his authority in Rome, but that overall he was not up in arms over the action – when in truth the Pope was anything but unmoved by the Nazis actions, and was working hard behind the scenes to save as many Jews as possible].

It is generally held that Weizsäcker's telegram was meant to help the Jews, but unfortunately it was also a gift to those with anti-Pius agendas.

3. *Pius XII, Hitler and the Jews*, J. Derek Holmes, Catholic Truth Society

CHAPTER XIV

"Il Papa, Il Papa!"

Even before the Allied landings in Sicily, in fact ever since Mussolini had dragged Italy into the war, Pius had been grimly aware of the dangers to the Vatican and to Rome. He urgently ordered air raid shelters to be built and special steel vaults were constructed in order to preserve the Vatican's priceless treasures.

Whilst every effort was being made to promote peace, Pius was also concerned to keep the war away from Rome itself. The issue became even more urgent after Italy entered the war on the side of the Axis, and the Luftwaffe began its systematic bombardment of London, and other major British cities.

After it was noted by the British government that Italian planes had been sent to bomb England, or so Mussolini boasted,* the matter became yet more urgent. The neutrality of the Vatican was recognised by the Allies but such was the lack of precision in high altitude bombing that any air raids on Rome were likely to see bombs fall on the Holy See, too. Besides, the Eternal City itself was the Pope's own diocese, it was replete with artistic and historic monuments and covered with sacred edifices that were venerated the world over. Any bombing raids would be a disaster in both human and cultural terms.

For a long time air raids did not materialise, but, after the Allied invasion of Italy, Allied aircraft carried out massive bombing raids on Genoa, Turin and Milan and the situation became intense.

---

* The planes never actually reached England.

The Pope began a feverish round of diplomatic discussions, sending numerous diplomatic notes, telegrams and cables in an effort to keep the Anglo-American bombers from targeting Rome. He requested that the Italian government remove all military targets from the city, but the governments remained intransigent and the option of bombing Rome was retained by the Allies as a legitimate tactic should the war effort warrant it.

It was soon decided to turn the bombers on Rome. On July 19th, between ten past eleven in the morning and three in the afternoon, some 500 Allied planes attacked the Roman train yard and its adjacent installations. Residential areas around the yards were also hit, as was the Basilica di San Lorenzo fuori le Mura and the nearby cemetery of Campo Verano, where the Pope's parents were buried. The number of victims has been estimated at some 1,500 killed and even more injured.

At the Vatican Pius watched the aircraft swoop over St. Peter's and heard the bombs fall. He immediately contacted Monsignor Montini and instructed him to withdraw all the cash that the Vatican Bank contained, some two million lira, and to meet him with a car immediately in the St. Damaso Courtyard.

The Pope and Montini jumped quickly into the car and sped off in the direction of the bombs. Within three minutes they were racing through the Piazza Venezia, turning into the Via Nazionale. The unescorted car screeched to a halt in the plaza in front of the railway station. Pius leapt from his car, to the amazement of the public in the plaza. Immediately the cry went up: "Il Papa, Il Papa!"

The people clustered around the Holy Father, clutching at his cassock. A workman threw his jacket down onto the cobblestones and the Pope and his people knelt to pray.[1]

Pius and Montini gave the last rites to many of the dying, and the Pope ordered that all the money be distributed to the needy. As Montini distributed the money a distraught mother thrust the body of her dead baby into the arms of the Holy Father. The Pope stood tenderly holding the child, trying to say what words of consolation he could. It was not until eight o'clock that evening that a shattered Pius, his white cassock stained with grime and blood, was finally driven back to the Vatican.

1. *Crown of Glory, The Life of Pope Pius XII,* by Alden Hatch and Seamus Walshe. Heinemann

The attacks continued to haunt Rome but on Mussolini's overthrow Pius sensed a chance to end the carnage. Pius suggested having Rome declared an open city. Badoglio and the King were favourable to the suggestion but the Allies were still wary and on August 13th, Rome was again raided. This time the bombs rained down on the district of San Giovanni near the Pope's own church of St. John Lateran. Once more Pius hurried to the scene, passing from one sorrowing group to another, heedless of his own safety. Once again his white cassock was covered with blood and his shoes cut by the broken glass. [1]

The next day, August 14th, Marshall Badoglio declared that Rome was an open city. On September 3rd an envoy from Marshall Badoglio, General Castellani, met with Eisenhower in Sicily and signed the armistice, which was to be made public once the Allies went ashore at Salerno. On September 8th Eisenhower announced the surrender of Italy and shortly afterwards Badoglio announced the same to the Italian people.

Hitler had foreseen this, and he acted swiftly. By the morning of September 10th the soldiers of Field Marshall Kesselring were just outside Rome. Pius ordered the Papal guards to store their plumed helmets and halberds, and arm themselves with rifles and machine guns, and on the morning of the 10th ordered the entrance to the Vatican at Porta Santa Anna to be sealed and the great doors of St. Peter's closed – the first time in its history that they had ever been shut in the daytime.

It was to no avail. There was sporadic fighting around the city and pockets of resistance fought the invaders but the confused and outnumbered Italian troops were no match for Hitler's Wehrmacht. The enemy poured into Rome, and the ancient streets echoed to the sound of their jackboots.

Earlier King Victor Emmanuel took what was probably the most disastrous step of his long reign when he, the Royal Family and part of the government, including Badoglio, fled Rome.* Pius, of course, remained and found himself directly facing the forces of the Reich.

---

1. *Crown of Glory, The Life of Pope Pius XII,* by Alden Hatch and Seamus Walshe. Heinemann

* Hitler had ordered the arrest of the King, his family and Badoglio, the decision to flee can be judged in the light of the need to protect the head of state and the government.

Pictured above,
Hitler and Mussolini

King Victor Emmanuel III

The Holy Father returns to the Vatican in April 1948, having addressed the crowds in St. Peter's Square ahead of the Italian General Election

Pope Pius XII broadcasts to the world on the occasion of the Coronation of the Image of Our Lady of Fatima on May 13th, 1946. Monsignor Montini, the future Pope Paul VI, stands to the left behind the Holy Father

Sisters of Charity of St. Vincent de Paul greet the Holy Father during an audience in St. Peter's June 1956

Addressing the Palatine Guard in the Belvedere Courtyard of the Vatican on the 100th anniversary of their foundation, July 1950

Pictured above,
Pope Pius XII is
welcomed to Castel
Gandolfo by the
town's mayor,
Marcello Costa
August 1954

The Marchesa
Elisabetta Rossignani
Pacelli, who was the
sole surviving
member of Pius'
immediate family,
arrives at Castel
Gandolfo in
October 1958 as the
Pope's condition
worsened

A general scene at the foot of the altar in the Basilica of St. Peter on October 13th, 1958 during the nine days of funeral ceremonies for Pope Pius XII

Pictured below,
A view of the final official Requiem Mass for the late Pope in St. Peter's Basilica on October 19th, 1958. The Papal Tiara sits atop the coffin

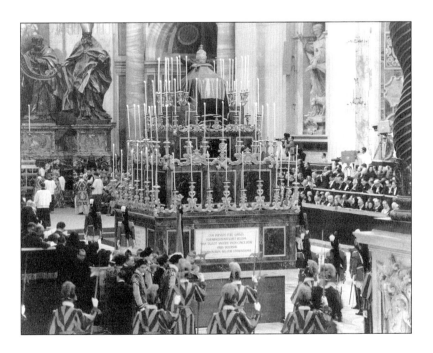

CHAPTER XV

"Urbi et Orbi"

The Vatican was now besieged. German sentries paced up and down just beyond St. Peter's Square and with the occupation came yet another concern for the Pope, how to keep the people of Rome, whose numbers were growing daily due to the influx of refugees, supplied with food and other necessities. It is estimated that 500,000 refugees had swelled the walls of the city by May 1944. Once again permission was given for them to shelter in basilicas, and churches – even under the colonnades around St. Peter's Square. But it was obvious that these people were facing starvation.

Pius acted quickly and sent out a fleet of vehicles clearly marked with a cross and the papal colours of yellow and white to scour the countryside for food. The first convoy returned with over 300,000 lbs of food. Soup kitchens were opened, with as many as 200,000 soup rations and 50,000 hot meals served by the Vatican everyday.

By this point in the war, however, Pius had given away virtually all the Vatican's cash, including his own money. To fund the relief effort a great "Crusade of Charity" was organised throughout the world.

On June 29th, 1943 the Holy Father published his encyclical, *Mystici Corporis*, on the Church as the mystical body of Christ. In it the Pope reflected on both the divine and the human natures of Christ, and on his infinite love for the whole of mankind. *Mystici Corporis* did not get much attention during the war years but became influential after World War II. It rejected two extreme views of the Church. A rationalistic or purely sociological understanding of the Church, according to which she is merely a human organisation with structures and activities. The visible Church and its structures do exist but the Church is more, she is guided by the Holy Spirit, said Pius. "Although the juridical principles on which the Church rests and is established derive from the divine constitution given to it by Christ and contribute to the attaining of its supernatural end, nevertheless that which lifts the Society of Christians far above the whole natural order is the Spirit of our Redeemer who penetrates and fills every part of the Church."[1]

He went on to complete his teaching on this encyclical with another, published on September 30th of the same year, called *Divino Afflante Spiritu* (Inspired by the Divine Spirit). This set out to promote biblical studies as the necessary means for a deeper and a truer understanding of God's revelation to mankind. In fact it inaugurated the modern period of Roman Catholic Bible studies by permitting the limited use of modern methods of biblical criticism. The Catholic Bible scholar, Raymond E. Brown, described it as a "Magna Carta for biblical progress."

In the meantime, Pius' efforts to save Rome and the people sheltered by her intensified. In January 1944 the outskirts of Rome began to suffer almost continuous bombing. Another diplomatic round of activity ensued as the Pope tried to get the Allies to agree to the cessation of the bombing. The replies were of a uniform nature: as long as the Germans were entrenched in Rome, then they would have to be driven out. Only if the Pope persuaded the Germans to vacate Rome could the city be spared the bombing raids.[2]

The Secretary of State, Cardinal Maglione, prepared a note that was sent to the German ambassador on March 11th. The note foresaw Rome becoming the centre of the fighting; so to spare Rome, a city which is "unique and incomparable in the political and cultural evolution of the human race and which has been the centre and mother of Christian civilisation for close to twenty centuries," would be an accomplishment for which Germany could take exceptional credit,[2] the note said.

On the 14th and 19th of March Rome was once again bombed, eliciting further protests from the Pope, but while he was trying to prevent further raids on Rome, an Italian resistance group exploded a bomb on the Via

1. Pius XII, Enc. *Mystici Corporis Christi*, 63
2. *Pius XII and the Second World War, According to the Archives of the Vatican*, Pierre Blet, S.J. Gracewing

Rasella, a narrow street in the city centre, as a column of German soldiers was passing by. 32 were killed and the German response was swift and brutal. The order arrived from the Nazi High Command, in Hitler's name, to execute ten Italians for every German who died, and to do so within 24 hours. Early in the hours of March 24th, 335 Italians, detained in various prisons for political reasons, some Jews and others, none of whom had anything to do with the attack – were taken out of the city to the Adreatine Caves where they were machine gunned by an SS squad commanded by the same Lt. Col. Kappler who had been in charge of rounding up the Jews of Rome after the gold ransom demand. The entrance to the caves was then dynamited, thus sealing their tombs; it was later discovered that some had been buried alive.

Gradually worldwide pressure began to grow in favour of saving the Eternal City, and in the end the Germans agreed to remove every military target from Rome. By the end of May the British Eighth Army had reached the Alban Hills and Allied soldiers could see the great dome of St. Peter's in the distance. Pius could hear the boom of Allied artillery. The atmosphere in Rome was unbearable, and the population seemed to take a collective intake of breath in anticipation of the future. But relief was near at hand: on June 2nd, 1944, the Germans started to leave. Both sides held to the agreement and as the German columns wound out of the northern gates, the British and Americans watched their departure. Rome was saved.

On June 4th American troops entered the Roman suburbs, and by seven that evening the American 88th Division arrived at the Piazza Venezia. A Jewish brigade officer serving in the US army was quoted in a Hebrew newspaper shortly afterwards as saying, "When we entered Rome, the Jewish survivors told us in a voice filled with deep gratitude and respect: 'if we have been rescued, if Jews are still alive in Rome, come with us and thank the Pope in the Vatican. For in the Vatican itself, in Churches, monasteries and private homes, Jews were kept hidden at his personal orders.'"[1]

At seven the following morning Pope Pius XII appeared at the window of his apartment in order to bless the crowd which had gathered. He repeated this three hours later, and at six that evening he appeared on

1. *Pius XII*, Ethel Tolansky and Helena Scott, CTS

the central balcony of the basilica. The previous day had seen the feast of the Holy Trinity, and it was to the Trinity that the Pope referred in his address of thanksgiving:

"In a spirit of praise and adoration and with a heart full of thanks, We raise Our mind and heart to the one triune God, to the Father to the Son, and to the Holy Ghost. It was on their solemn feast day, and with divine mercy inspiring both belligerent parties with considerations of peace and not of affliction, that the Eternal City was preserved from incommensurable danger."[1]

And once again he gave his blessing, *Urbi et Orbi*, to the city and the world.

1. *Pius XII and the Second World War, According to the Archives of the Vatican*, Pierre Blet, S.J. Gracewing

CHAPTER XVI

"The people of Israel will never forget..."

As we have seen, Pius' work on behalf of the Jews of Europe was rendered next to useless when dealing directly with the Nazis. Their intransigence tended to render papal interventions as virtually predestined to failure.

Earlier in the war, however, the Holy Father had pursued an alternative strategy. He realised that papal interventions aimed at the Axis satellite states, namely Slovakia, Croatia, Rumania and Hungary were more likely to succeed.

Towards the end of 1941, predominantly Catholic Slovakia, under the influence of the Germans, promulgated an anti-Semitic code. But Slovakia was not Germany. In fact, uniquely, its president, Josef Tiso, was a priest. As soon as the anti-Jewish regulations were announced the Vatican, through its nunciature in Bratislava, protested. The Holy See had to wait six months for a reply and when it arrived was told that the question of the code was no longer relevant as Slovakia intended to solve its "problem" by means of deportation. It had been decided to deport some 80,000 Jews regardless of sex, age, or even religion to Poland where they would be at the mercy of the Germans. It was tantamount to a death sentence.

Despite Vatican protestations, many of them on the direct authority of Pius himself, the deportations began in early 1942. Pius, through

Secretary of State Maglione and the nunciature continued to intervene until finally the deportations were halted between October 1942 and September 1944.

It wasn't the only country where the Pope tried to intervene on behalf of the Jews. As Rome was liberated the Pope was also fighting a desperate battle to save the Jews of Hungary, who were now being deported to the concentration camps. He appealed directly to the Regent of Hungary, Admiral Horthy, and for a while the persecutions slackened. However, in October of 1944 Horthy himself was arrested, the Nazis took direct power and the deportations began again. The Pope had help in his plans however. Among his most capable helpers was an archbishop called Angelo Rotta, the Apostolic Nuncio in Budapest. During his previous diplomatic activity in Bulgaria he had already saved many Bulgarian Jews by issuing them baptismal certificates and safe conducts for the trip to Palestine.

Between 1944 and 1945 Rotta issued at least 15,000 protection letters to Hungarian Jews and provided them with baptismal certificates. On behalf of the Pope and as the Dean of the Diplomatic Corps, he vehemently protested several times to the Hungarian Government against the Jewish deportations.

Also prominent in rescue attempts was the apostolic delegate in Istanbul, Angelo Roncalli, later Pope John XXIII. Roncalli later referred to the virtual obliteration of European Jewry as "six million crucifixions," and commented, "In all these painful matters I have referred to the Holy See and simply carried out the Pope's orders: first and foremost to save Jewish lives."

Such efforts to save Jews did not go unnoticed. On December 1st, 1944 the World Jewish Congress sent a telegram of thanks to the Holy See for the protection it had afforded [under very difficult circumstances] to the persecuted Jews in Hungary.

And this compliment was the first of many. As the war moved to its conclusion, similar messages and expressions of gratitude to Pope Pius XII poured into the Vatican from all over the world. The Chief Rabbi of Palestine, Isaac Herzog, said: "The people of Israel will never forget what

His Holiness and his illustrious delegates inspired by the eternal principles of religion which form the very foundation of true civilisation, are doing for our unfortunate brothers and sisters in the most tragic hour of our history, which is living proof of Divine Providence in this world."

On April 7th, 1944, Chief Rabbi Alexander Safran, of Bucharest, Rumania, presented the following statement to Monsignor Andrea Cassulo, Papal Nuncio to the county: "In the most difficult hours which we Jews of Rumania have passed through, the generous assistance of the Holy See was decisive and salutary. It is not easy for us to find the right words to express the warmth and consolation we experience because of the concern of the Supreme Pontiff, who offered a large sum to relieve the sufferings of deported Jews which had been pointed out to him by you after your visit to Transnistria. The Jews of Rumania will never forget these facts of historic importance."

In the summer of 1945, a petition was presented to Pope Pius XII by 20,000 Jewish refugees from Central Europe: "Allow us to ask the great honour of being able to thank, personally, His Holiness for the generosity he has shown us when we were being persecuted during the terrible period of Nazi-Fascism."

At the end of World War II, Dr. Joseph Nathan, representing a Hebrew Commission, expressed his heartfelt gratitude to those who protected and saved Jews during the Nazi-Fascist persecutions. "Above all," he said in an address to the Jewish community, "we acknowledge the Supreme Pontiff and the religious men and women who, executing the directives of the Holy Father, recognised the persecuted as their brothers and, with great abnegation, hastened to help them, disregarding the terrible dangers to which they were exposed." (*L'Osservatore Romano*, September 8th, 1945).

And, of course, most famously, the Chief Rabbi of Rome, Dr. Israel Zolli, converted to Catholicism after the war. In tribute to the Pope he took the name "Eugenio."

CHAPTER XVII

" ...most esteemed and venerated man"

Any new study of the life of Pope Pius XII is now, to a large extent, always overshadowed by the myth of his silence during the Second World War. The natural corollary being that people give scant attention to his pontificate post-1945.

This is to do the Holy Father a great disservice. For, after 1945, his determination to tackle the evils of communism, his handling of the Cold War, along with his teaching, theological and pastoral work are worthy of studies in themselves.

This book encompasses the formative years of Eugenio Pacelli, culminating in his reactions to and actions during the Second World War, and then looks at the growth of the anti-Pacelli industry. What it most certainly does not intend to do is to either demean or ignore the work that he did as supreme pontiff between 1945 and 1958, but which must, as space dictates, be in a shortened form.

For clearly the end of the Second World War did not end the challenges facing Pius XII, and Fascism and Nazism were not the only threats that Pope Pius XII had to deal with. Early in the war he had correctly foreseen the perils of atheistic communism.

In the countries behind the Iron Curtain, Stalin began his systematic eradication of all religion, with a special hatred reserved for the Catholic

Church. The Church refused to submit meekly to communist threats, but all too often their resistance was met with savage reprisals, as in the case of Cardinal Joszef Mindszenty of Hungary. Mindszenty had been ardently anti-Nazi during the war, and had in fact been imprisoned by the Germans. Ironically, the Russians freed him. But from 1946 onwards the cardinal became the greatest thorn in the Hungarian Communists' side.

Eventually he was arrested. In December 1948, at midnight, police cars surrounded the cardinal's house. He heard the crunch of jackboots on the gravel, and a crash as the front door was smashed open. It was a familiar scene to the cardinal, except that the swastikas had been replaced with red stars.

He was accused of every crime that the communists could think of: treason, currency fraud, black market dealing, even spying on behalf of the Americans.

Pius publicly denounced the whole sham and called a special assembly of the sacred Consistory of Cardinals to discuss the Church's approach to the persecutions in the Eastern Bloc.

The story of communist persecution was the same in every country that the Russians controlled. Across the Adriatic from Rome in Yugoslavia Marshal Josip Tito was also attempting to suppress the Church. Worryingly, the Pope faced communist opposition at home, too, with the threat of a communist victory in the forthcoming Italian general election of 1948.

Bound by the Lateran treaties Pius was prevented from entering into Italian party politics but he pushed the bounds as far as he could, ensuring that everyone in Italy read or heard his views, repeatedly warning against the dangers of the communists winning power. The communists failed to achieve their predicted victory, and part of the reason can fairly be put down to Pope Pius XII.

The Pope did not stop there either, and in 1949 a decree of the Holy Office against communism was published, and in the Apostolic letter *Carissimis Russiae populis* (July 7th, 1952) the Pope made a point, however, of distinguishing between the communist-Bolshevik system, and the Russian people.

On November 1st, 1950, which he had declared a Holy Year, Pius solemnly proclaimed the dogma of the Assumption:

"By the authority of our Lord Jesus Christ, of the Blessed Apostles Peter and Paul, and by our own authority, We pronounce, declare, and define it to be a divinely revealed dogma: that the Immaculate Mother of God, the ever Virgin Mary, having completed the course of her earthly life, was assumed body and soul into heavenly glory."

The dogma of the bodily assumption of the Virgin Mary has been described as the crowning of the theology of Pius XII. In this dogmatic statement, the phrase "having completed the course of her earthly life," leaves open the question of whether the Virgin Mary died before her Assumption, or whether she was assumed before death; both possibilities are allowed. Mary's Assumption was a divine gift to Mary as Mother of God.

In 1954 the Pope's health, never strong, began to falter, and his exhausting working practices had to be curtailed. Long ceremonies were avoided, as were any arduous journeys. It was also during this period that Pius began to promote young priests to the episcopate, such as Julius Döpfner (35 years) and Karol Wojtyla (38 years), one of his last appointees in 1958. He also took a firm stand against pastoral experiments, such as 'worker-priests,' who worked full-time in factories and joined political parties and unions. As always he continued to defend the theological tradition of Thomism as worthy of continued reform, and as superior to modern trends such as phenomenology or existentialism.

He also continued to write, publishing four encyclicals, and made many addresses, including one on the subject of television, in which whilst pointing out its advantages, he also drew attention to its dangers. Reading it today the ideas it contains are as apt now as they were then.

In the last years of his pontificate Pius increasingly addressed the laity and interest groups throughout the world on an unprecedented range of topics. He spoke frequently to members of scientific bodies, explaining Christian teachings in the light of the most recent scientific findings. This fascination with science, and its underlying relationship with eternal truth, is an aspect of Pius' life and pontificate that has always been under estimated, but which blossomed during these twilight years. Closely linked to this was his interest in medical ethics and during his later years he was happy to answer specific medical questions which were addressed to him by a number of professional associations, to whom he explained specific occupational ethics in the light of the faith and Church teachings.

And it was thus, although weakened and increasingly frail but still intellectually strong, that Pius continued on into the nineteenth year of his pontificate.

The end when it did come was sudden.

On Sunday, October 5th, 1958, Eugenio was at Castel Gandolfo. Three times during the day he braved a chill wind to go outside. On one occasion he spoke for 20 minutes to a congress of international notaries in the open courtyard of the palace, then in the afternoon took a stroll in the garden, and later appeared at a window to bless the hundreds of pilgrims who gathered in the courtyard each Sunday. On the following day he suffered a stroke. Despite being plagued by constant illness since 1954, it seemed at one stage as if he would make a good recovery, and by Tuesday it was reported that he had regained consciousness, was lucid, and had full use of his limbs. There were concerns, however, about possible complications, and kidney trouble. The Last Rites were administered, although Vatican officials described this as a precaution, adding that although his condition was serious he was in fact rallying. At 8.15am on the Wednesday the Holy Father asked for Holy Communion, and one of the priests attached to the private library was vesting when the Pope fell into a coma. The priest gave Eugenio Absolution, as Extreme Unction had already been administered, and soon the world heard the news that Pope Pius XII was dying.

The Vatican notified cardinals and nuncios throughout the world. Cardinal Tisserant, dean of the Sacred College of Cardinals, immediately flew back to Rome from a holiday in France, and other cardinals began to gather at Castel Gandolfo. His sister Elisabetta, now a widow, and his three nephews, Princes Carlo, Marcantonio and Giulio Pacelli, also arrived, and the world waited.

The village of Castel Gandolfo, with its population of 5,000 suddenly became the centre of a vast network of communications, flashing news instantly to the nations of the world.

As dusk fell the drama continued in the Pope's second floor bedroom. A light shone from the window and in the village square the recitation of the rosary could be heard.

At 2.52am Eugenio Pacelli, Pope Pius XII, with his sister and three nephews at his bedside, died peacefully.

Four minutes later Vatican Radio broadcast the news to the world, and in a voice breaking with emotion Fr. Francesco Pellegrini, commented: "He was the most esteemed and venerated man in the world, and the greatest Pope of the century."

Before he had lost consciousness his final words had been, "Pray, pray that this regrettable situation for the Church may end."

The bells of Castel Gandolfo's small church of St. Sebastian began to toll, and from a mast at the palace the papal flag was run up to fly at half-mast.

CHAPTER XVIII

" ...a Christ-like sanctity of spirit"

Only passing bells, tolling sadly from Rome's churches, broke the silence which fell on a million people as they watched Eugenio Giuseppe Giovanni Pacelli go home for the last time.

As his body left the little hill town of Castel Gandolfo soon after midday on Friday, October 10th, the hot autumn sun shone on the crowds packing the square in front of the papal palace.

Glass-sided, its four corners surmounted by gilt angels, with a replica of the papal tiara on the top, the hearse was escorted by 40 Italian police motor cyclists. Ten cars followed it with Vatican dignitaries and close relatives. Monsignor Pietro Canisio Van Lierde, sacristan to the Pope was in one of the open cars at the head of the procession. He and a second priest held large gilt crucifixes.

The 14-mile journey from the Alban Hills back to Rome was made almost without ceremony, the cars driving at a steady 20 miles an hour. Peasants blessed themselves in the fields, and all along the road the carabinieri stood with heads bowed and hands clasped over glittering ceremonial swords.

Then the city was reached, the city the Pope had loved and saved from destruction. Troops lined the streets and along the route shops were shuttered, Italian tricolours flew at half-mast, and on the walls and public notice boards sombre black-edged posters proclaimed, *"Il Papa e morto."*

The last three miles were through the heart of the city. At St. John Lateran, the cathedral of the diocese of Rome, the Pontiff received the last absolutions for the Ordinary of the See.

When the cortege reached St. Peter's the last rays were glowing copper-red off the gigantic Michelangelo cupola of the basilica. The simple cypress coffin was lifted down, the great bronze doors swung open, and under the glare of television lamps, escorted by the Noble Guards, members of Rome's greatest families, the Pope was borne into his cathedral.

Thus did Pope Pius XII enter St. Peter's for the last time. The Supreme Pontiff for 19 years, he was known throughout the world, his image more familiar than that of any other Pope in history, but who was this man? He left no memoir, he kept no diary, that we know of, we have only the recollections of people who knew him – but there is the difficulty. "People who knew him." Many knew Pius on the surface but no one really knew him intimately. He had no intimate friends.

Domenico Tardini, his sub-Secretary of State and later Secretary of State under John XXIII, wrote a short appreciation of Pius shortly after the Pope's death. Pius, Tardini said, was mild and shy, not a fighter – unlike Pius XI, who relished a battle. He preferred solitude, and this "disposed him to avoid rather than face the battles of life." He tried to please everyone and believed the best of everyone. When he had to write a criticism of someone, he 'sugar-pilled' his response so as to avoid offending.[1]

Pius, from the earliest days, saw the potential of the radio, and later television, and he embraced both mediums with open arms. With his tall, gaunt and ethereal looks he easily became everyone's ideal of a Pope. Raised in the embattled world of the 'Black Nobility,' he had early on decided that, if given the chance, he would raise the Church to its rightful place in the world, including all the trappings and splendour of that One Holy Catholic and Apostolic Church. And this he certainly did. It is thus easy to see how Pius and his pontificate attracted adulation from many.

Adulation, though, has its problems and stemming from such adulation sprang many an idiotic tale. At the outbreak of war it was reported widely

---

1. *Pius XII and the Holocaust,* Jose M.Sanchez, CUA Press

that the Holy Father slept "on the floor [so] that he may participate more deeply in the world's suffering." The Vatican issued a prompt denial, noting that if the Pope were making such sacrifices, he would not be making the fact public.[2]

Some of his reported sacrifices were accurate, however Tardini does tell us that during the war, "Pius gave out his own food, multiplied his penances, and did not want his apartment to be heated in the severe winter." Such sacrifice had its effect: by the end of the war, he had only eight stone on his six-foot frame.[3]

He had also given away virtually the whole of his personal wealth by the end of his pontificate.

That Pius was deeply spiritual has never been doubted, and this spirituality must always be taken into account when trying to evaluate his personality – all who knew him testify to it. A typical observation was: "I was always captivated by the incomparable charm of Pius XII's intensely spiritual personality," Ernst von Weizsäcker, 1943.

He also had an enormous devotion to Our Lady and a belief in the power of Her intercessions. On May 13th, 1942, the Silver Jubilee of his ordination he had dedicated the whole human race to Mary's Immaculate Heart, assigning a special feast day in honour of the Queenship of Mary.

Pius also witnessed the Fatima-like "miracles of the sun" four times, which was confirmed as recently as 2008 in a handwritten, unpublished note from Pius, discovered in the Pacelli family archives.

It describes the "miracle of the sun," an episode that had only previously been affirmed by the indirect testimony of Cardinal Federico Tedeschini (1873-1959), who recounted in a homily that the Holy Father had seen the miracle.

Pius XII wrote, "I have seen the 'miracle of the sun,' this is the pure truth."

The miracle of the sun occurred in Fatima, Portugal, on October 13th, 1917 when, according to the Fatima visionaries, Our Blessed Lady had said there would be a miracle that day so that people would come to believe. Thousands had gathered at the site of the visions, and the sun "danced," reportedly drying instantaneously the rain-soaked land and spectators.

2. *New York Times*, September 19th, 1939
3. *Memories of Pius XII*, Cardinal Tardini

Pius XII's note says that he saw the miracle in the year he was to proclaim the dogma of the Assumption, 1950, while he walked in the Vatican Gardens. He also said he saw the phenomenon at various times, considering it a confirmation of his plan to declare the dogma. The papal note says that at 4pm on October 30th, 1950, during his "habitual walk in the Vatican Gardens, reading and studying," having arrived at the statue of Our Lady of Lourdes, "toward the top of the hill... I was awestruck by a phenomenon that before now I had never seen."

"The sun, which was still quite high, looked like a pale, opaque sphere, entirely surrounded by a luminous circle," he recounted. And one could look at the sun, "without the slightest bother. There was a very light little cloud in front of it."

Pius' note goes on to describe "the opaque sphere" that "moved outward slightly, either spinning, or moving from left to right and vice versa. But within the sphere, you could see marked movements with total clarity and without interruption."

Pius XII said he saw the same phenomenon "on October 31st and November 1st, the day of the definition of the dogma of the Assumption, and then again on November 8th, and after that, no more."

The Pope acknowledged that on other days at about the same hour, he tried to see if the phenomenon would be repeated, "but in vain – I couldn't fix my gaze [on the sun] for even an instant; my eyes would be dazzled."[4]

Pius' spirituality also saw its natural outlet in his teachings. His oral allocutions alone numbered over 1,000, which surpassed those of any of his predecessors. He also issued 41 encyclicals during his pontificate – more than all his successors in the past 50 years taken together – along with many other writings and speeches. The pontificate of Pius XII was the first in Vatican history which published papal speeches and addresses in vernacular language on a systematic basis.

Pius was a man who touched many who met him, including those from outside the Church. "I never expected to meet a saint who radiated goodness and serenity. I met that saint," these were the words of David Gray, one-time American Minister to Ireland and a non-Catholic after a meeting with Pope Pius XII.

4. *Pius XII Saw "Miracle of the Sun"* (Zenit, 4/11/08)

Another non-Catholic, Myron Taylor, President Roosevelt's personal representative to the Pope, and a Quaker, paid this tribute: "In him we can have a supreme confidence, founded solidly not only on his holy office, but also on his embracing spirituality, his vision and his very great talent."

Another side to Pius was seen by Cardinal Spellman of America, and shows clearly the strain that the war had taken on the Pope. Nearly three years after the war had ended, he wrote to his diocese that the Pope was, "aged, thin, and saddened," since he last saw him, and went on: "No robust physical stature nor strong broad shoulders has the Pope to bear the sorrow of the world, but the Christ-like figure, and the Christ-like shoulders, and a Christ-like sanctity of spirit seems to characterise him."[5]

5. *The Universe,* October 10th, 1958

CHAPTER XIX

"Where the Pope wants to cry out loud..."

For his peace efforts prior to the Second World War, for his actions and comments during that war, and then for nearly 13 years afterwards, Pope Pius XII was regarded as a virtual saint. No other Pope in history had been so universally praised by the Jewish people, both during his lifetime and at his death.

By the 1960s, however, like a slow working poison, a campaign of vilification against the memory of Pius XII had begun to work its way into the public perception of Eugenio Pacelli.

He began to be attacked for his alleged failure to speak out against Hitler during the Holocaust, and his alleged "silence" in the face of the worst Nazi atrocities. His harshest critics went further, accusing him of being a Nazi sympathiser or an actual anti-Semite.

The detractors' strategy was a simple one. Ignore the facts and re-write history. As Sr. Margherita Marchione points out in her book, *Pope Pius XII, Architect for Peace*, the accusers ignore the reality of who had the power and the will to destroy mercilessly from 1933 to 1944, and to pretend that Pius XII possessed some kind of extraordinary ability that no one else in the world had – to make Hitler obey him.[1]

The campaign of vilification against Pope Pius can largely be traced to the opening of a play in Berlin in February 1963, written by a young

---

1. *Pope Pius XII, Architect for Peace*, Margherita Marchione, Paulist Press

Protestant, left-wing West German writer and playwright, Rolf Hochhuth. This purely fictional work, entitled *The Deputy*, portrays Pope Pius XII as a Nazi collaborator. It offers not one jot of historical evidence in its attack on Pius. It is set in the Second World War and the plot is based around a real character, an SS officer called Kurt Gerstein, and a fictional Jesuit priest, Riccardo Fontana. Pius XII is portrayed as a compassionless, cold and detached figure, who cares nothing for the fate of the Jews and refuses to denounce the Nazis out of moral cowardice and fear of damaging the Vatican's imagined "financial interests" abroad.

As matter of interest Hochhuth also wrote a play about Winston Churchill. In the play a pilot was said to have sabotaged a plane containing a high-ranking Polish officer. Hochhuth was sued and forced to pay considerable damages to the British government, and to the pilot, who was found to be living in California.

The Pius play was totally second-rate but the seeds were sown. According to Robert A. Graham, the Jesuit historian, Pius became a villain, not on historical grounds but for psychological reasons. In a lecture delivered at the Catholic University of America on October 10th, 1989, he suggested several hypotheses: "The most important is the timing. The first session of the historic Vatican Council had terminated just a few months previously. A new vision dawned not only on the Catholic Church, but also on world opinion. This was also the time when America was deeply troubled in conscience by the drama, the tragedy of the Vietnam War. Also, just two years previously the trial of Adolf Eichmann, the organiser of the Hitlerian programme for the extermination of the Jews, had taken place." Someone needed to be blamed for the Holocaust.[1]

Many of the attacks were without a doubt also inspired by communist propaganda which had consistently accused the Church and the members of its hierarchy of having collaborated with Hitler and the Nazis before and during the war, because of their fear of communism. Pius had seen atheistic communism at first hand and had constantly fought against it with every weapon at his disposal throughout his life. The communists now sought their revenge and he came under special attack from their propaganda machine.

1. *Pope Pius XII, Architect for Peace,* Margherita Marchione, Paulist Press

In an attempt to counter the attacks Pope Paul VI (the former Cardinal Montini) over-ruled the Vatican time restraints on the release of archives, (70 years) and the archives relating to the activities of Pope Pius XII and the Church between the years 1939 and 1945 were released. Three Jesuit Church historians took up the challenge of sifting and researching the many thousands of documents – Pierre Blet, Angelo Martini, and Burkhart Schneider – and in 1967 American Jesuit Robert A.Graham joined them.

Fr. Thomas Stransky, an original staff member of the Vatican Secretariat for Christian Unity (1960-1970), describing this work with the archives, points out that the researchers' aim was not to order and index the entire massive documentation but to select what they judged to pertain to Pius XII and his Secretariat of State during World War II.

Their work resulted in 12 volumes completed between 1965 and 1981. [2]

The volumes were neither sanitised nor interpreted, and equally the motives of its chief characters are not interpreted either. Fr. Pierre Blet, eventually published a complementation and interpretation of this original work in 1997. Throughout he used very few other archival sources.

It is worth looking at Fr. Stransky's preface to this work in which he quotes an address Pius made to nurses in May 1952, in which he asked himself; "What should we have done that we have not done?" Pierre Blet judges that "insofar as the documents allow anyone to probe the human heart of another," they do support the same conclusion of Pius XII regarding these years of fire and sword: "He was conscious of what he had done to prevent the war, to alleviate sufferings, to reduce the number of its victims, everything he thought he could do." The Pope saw himself between contradictory pastoral demands; "reserve and prudent silence, or resolutely speaking out and vigorous action." As Pius wrote in February 1941 to the German bishops: "Where the Pope wants to cry out loud and strong, it is expectation in silence that are unhappily imposed on him; where he would act and give assistance, it is patience and waiting [that are imposed]." [3]

This succinctly sums up the dilemma that faced Pius during those years of war and fits well with Paul VI's statement in defence of the Holy Father. The former Cardinal Montini had been one of Pius' closest advisors, and thus his testimony was particularly significant.

2. *Actes et Documents du Saint Siege relatifs a la Seconde Guerre Mondiale,* published by the Vatican Press
3. *Pius XII and the Second World War, According to the Archives of the Vatican,* Pierre Blet, S.J. Gracewing

Montini had been archbishop of Milan since the end of 1954, and was made cardinal by John XXIII in 1958. His statement came in the form of an article in defence of Pius XII, published in *The Tablet* on May 11th, 1963. Amongst other things, it underlined the similarity between Hochhuth's play and a "communist publication" on the Vatican and the Second World War.

In a letter that reached *The Tablet* on June 21st, 1963, on the same day as he was elected Pope, the cardinal of Milan defended Pius XII's behaviour in the face of the persecution and extermination of Jews by the Nazis...

"This attitude of condemnation and protest, for the absence of which the Pope is being reproached, would not only have been futile, it would also have been dangerous."

He concluded: "Subjects like these and historic people we know should not be played with through the creative imagination of playwrights, who are lacking in historic discernment and, God help us, human honesty. Otherwise, just like in the present case, the drama would be another: that of someone trying to offload the horrible crimes of German Nazism onto a Pope who was extremely conscientious in his duties and aware of history, and who in the opinion of more than one friend was certainly impartial, but also very loyal to the German people. Equally, Pius XII had the merit of having been a 'Vicar' of Christ who tried to fulfil his mission as best he could with courage and integrity. Could the same thing be said of this theatrical injustice, in the context of culture and art?"

The defence of Pius' reputation was now gathering, and proceedings for his beatification were begun by Pope Paul in 1965.

CHAPTER XX

" *...Christ-like shoulders* "

When one sees and reads the world's tributes on the death of Pope Pius XII some 52 years after the event it invokes a painful nostalgia. The press, the radio, and the television of the day all made it abundantly clear that the late Pope had an international status and position that was unequalled at the time.

How different today. The iniquitous campaign of vilification has done its damage and mention of his name now causes controversy; dare mention beatification and the whole anti-Pacelli machine moves up a gear.

The damage can be repaired, and will be. Many ordinary people, many scholars and many holy men and women are dedicated to restoring the reputation of Eugenio Pacelli. Their weapon? Just one, the truth.

The main attacks and resulting damage always revolve around the Holy Father's conduct during the Second World War, but what still remains intact, virtually unassailable and largely undimmed is the recognition of Pius' saintly character, his spirituality and his devotion to the priesthood.

Once he had discerned his calling, his predilection was always to be a pastor. He yearned and prayed to be allowed to serve his Lord in the care of souls. His prayers were answered, but not in the manner he sought. He was granted a care of souls, not just over a Roman parish, but the whole world.

I do believe that he will go down in history as one of the greatest of the pontiffs. Slightly built, and ethereal in looks, he nonetheless managed to shoulder the very heaviest of burdens. That he did so was because he had been granted, in the words of Cardinal Spellman, "Christ-like shoulders" and had, "a Christ-like sanctity of spirit."

Venerable Pope Pius XII, Ora Pro Nobis.

INDEX

INDEX

BIBLIOGRAPHY

Blet, Pierre S.J., *Pius XII and the Second World War, from the Vatican Archives*, Leominster, 2003.

Cornwell, J., *Hitler's Pope*, Viking, 1999.

Frain John, *The Cross and The Third Reich*, Family Publications, 2009.

Gallo, Patrick J., (editor) *Pius XII, The Holocaust and the Revisionists*, McFarland and Co., 2006.

Hatch, Alden and Walshe, Seamus, *Crown of Glory*, Heinemann, 1957.

Holmes, J. Derek, *Pius XII, Hitler and the Jews*, CTS, 1982.

Holmes, J. Derek, *The Papacy in the Modern World*, Messrs Burns and Oates, 1981.

Kirkpatrick, Ivone, *The Inner Circle*, Macmillan, 1959.

Knox, Ronald, *Nazi and Nazarine*, (Macmillan War Pamphlets, No 5) London, 1940.

Lapide, Pinchas W., *The Last Three Popes and the Jews*, London, 1967.

Marchione, Margherita, *Pope Pius XII: Architect for Peace*, Paulist Press, 2000.

McGraw-Hill Book Co., *New Catholic Encyclopaedia*, 1966.

Murphy Paul I, and Arlington R. Rene, *La Popessa*, New York, 1983.

Noel, Gerard, *Pius XII, The Hound of Hitler*, Continuum, 2008.

Phayer, Michael, *Pius XII, The Holocaust and the Cold War*, Indiana, 2008.

Randall, Sir Alec, *The Pope, the Jews, and the Nazis*, CTS, 1963.

Sánchéz, José M., *Pius XII and the Holocaust, Understanding the Controversy*, CUA Press, 2002.

Shirer, William L., *The Rise and Fall of the Third Reich*, Simon & Schuster, 1995 edn.

Tardini, D., *Pius XII*, 1959.

Tolansky, Ethel and Scott, Helena, *Pius XII*, CTS, London 2003.